PRAISE FOR
Martha Pullen's Southern Family Cookbook

"'Who are your people?' is a question often uttered upon meeting a new acquaintance in the South, where family is life and stories about family, faith, and food are a treasured heritage. Authors Dr. Martha Campbell Pullen and Suzanne Crocker have given readers a gracious invitation to get to know "their people" through this book while drawing a blueprint for family history documentation: recording stories of family heritage and faith and creating family memories through cherished recipes. Readers will find themselves taking a stroll down memory lane as they read and cook, remembering their own family food heritage or resolving to create one. These easy-to-prepare recipes could easily become favorites of your family, resulting in that annual discussion at the Thanksgiving table years from now about how 'Mama's dressing is the best.'"

—Rhonda Edge Buescher, Director, Media Business Development,
LifeWay Christian Resources

"Martha Pullen epitomizes the southern hostess. Whether she is serving family or friends, she makes everyone her special guests. Her table is laden with her favorite dishes. She serves with the heart of a servant who is called by God to love and serve others."

—Phyllis Hoffman DePiano, President, Hoffman Media

"From the moment I met Martha, we were friends. She is an excellent writer, a good person, and best of all, a true friend. And her food is delicious!"

—Jude Deveraux, *New York Times* Bestselling Author

"Every cookbook should be more than pages filled with great recipes. It should be filled with recipes that bring to mind your favorite memory of your grandmother as she picked the fruit from the trees to make your favorite dessert, or your mother when she made your favorite birthday dinner. That is exactly what Martha's must-have cookbook gives to each of you: a much loved recipe, a treasured memory, and a time to spend in the heart of the home with loved ones while you both cook your meals and share them."

—Jo Packham, Editor-in-Chief, *Where Women Create and Where Women Cook*

"Your cookbook is fabulous . . . the recipes are wonderfully delicious and the stories are delightful. It is a must have for anyone's life and kitchen."

—LaQuinta Schum, Owner, Let's Sew, Evansville, IN

"I am 'sew' excited about Martha's new cookbook! Herb and I have visited Martha and Joe's home and they are wonderful hosts and serve fabulous food! It will be wonderful to have all her favorite recipes at my fingertips! On my first visit to Martha's home I had never heard of Chess Pie. Two slices later I was on a quest to find the recipe, and my Dad and I made it for every family occasion until his passing."

—Sue Hausmann, Host of *America Sews with Sue Hausmann*

"After thumbing through Martha's cookbook I found myself thinking about the many cookbooks and recipes my dad had given me from my grandmother who I never knew; however, when I would open them I could feel that we had some type of a connection through them. The many hours that Martha and Suzanne have spent compiling these recipes is truly an inspiration to all of us; it feeds our bodies, minds, and souls to overflowing. It will bring tears of joy to your eyes as you read the stories of their journey to this place in their lives and know we will feast at the eternal table forever. I love you Martha and thank you for all you have given us."

—Pamela Mahshie, Baby Lock USA's National Ambassador of Education

"Martha Pullen is the quintessential Southern matriarch—she is happiest when her home, and her dining table, are full of loved ones sharing a delicious meal. This book is an homage to all of the other Southern matriarchs in Martha's family who shared their recipes and stories with Martha. And what a treasure that she is now sharing them with us! This cookbook will inspire you to pick up a spatula and a pen because you will want to record your own stories as you try Martha and Suzanne's amazing recipes. Martha has amassed a business empire worthy of the biggest mogul. She has amassed that empire because she practices what she preaches—she lives her life and conducts her business by staying true to the Christian principles that have guided her family for generations. Through her personal recollections, we are able to see what makes a great cook, a great hostess, a great mother, and a great business woman—it's her ability to find joy in the simple things like a good meal, her adherence to the Christian principles that she lives by, and her willingness to share her knowledge and experience with others. Thank you, Martha and Suzanne, for this cookbook, which has inspired me to explore the great matriarchs, and their great recipes, in my own family."

—Debra Jenkins, Cofounder of the Merrimack Hall Performing Arts Center

Martha Pullen's Southern Family Cookbook

Reflect on the Past, Rejoice in the Present, and Celebrate Future
Gatherings with More Than 250 Heirloom Recipes & Meals

Martha Campbell Pullen & Suzanne Crocker

Avon, Massachusetts

Published by
Adams Media, a division of F+W Media, Inc.
57 Littlefield Street, Avon, MA 02322. U.S.A.
www.adamsmedia.com

ISBN 10: 1-4405-5007-7
ISBN 13: 978-1-4405-5007-2
eISBN 10: 1-4405-5008-5
eISBN 13: 978-1-4405-5008-9

Printed in the United States of America.

10   9   8   7   6   5   4   3   2   1

Always follow safety and common-sense cooking protocol while using kitchen utensils, operating ovens and stoves, and handling uncooked food. If children are assisting in the preparation of any recipe, they should always be supervised by an adult.

Photography: Kelly Jaggers

This book is available at quantity discounts for bulk purchases.
For information, please call 1-800-289-0963.

Dedication

This book is lovingly dedicated to the women in our families who taught us to cook, spent a lifetime preparing good food, passed down recipes, and created memories that warm their families' hearts with love. It is dedicated to our children and grandchildren and all future generations of our family with the prayer that they cherish the cooking genealogy recorded in this book and endeavor to make the same memories for their families. Finally, it is dedicated to the women and men who, by reading this book, are inspired to organize and sort out their own family recipes and stories to record for their loved ones. We send our love to all of you.

Acknowledgments

First, we would like to thank all the people who made this book possible, and made it look so beautiful!

Thank you to our editor, Katie Corcoran Lytle. You are a joy to work with, and we could not have done it without you! Bob Johnson, your cakes are absolutely amazing; you are the most creative cake designer in the world. Jennifer Tarkington, your photography never ceases to amaze and thrill me. Patty Smith, thank you for your help in getting the photography "props" together and in helping me find the right clothes for the photo. Amelia Johanson, thank you for your magic words in helping edit the first edition. To all of our family members and friends who gathered requested recipes together, thank you. Thanks to Sydney and Glenn Toups for the beautiful flower arrangements that I needed at the last minute. To Kelly Jaggers who cooked and photographed the food pictures, you are fabulous. To Suzanne's husband John and to Martha's husband Joe who actually did without creative meals while we wrote this book—you are the best! Your patience and encouragement is always with us. As in all things the first and most important acknowledgment is to thank God who allowed the whole book to happen. To God be the glory. Forever.

CONTENTS

CHAPTER 3

Beef & Pork 116

INTRODUCTION

The cooking members of my family have a lot in common with Jesus. Jesus gathered around the table with all sorts of people. The New Testament in the Bible tells about Jesus eating with tax collectors, sinners, drunkards, and gluttons. He shared meals with people from all walks of life, with both the poor and the wealthy. When a crowd followed him to a mountainside and listened to him all day, he wasn't willing to send them away hungry. He took a small boy's lunch, blessed it, broke it into pieces, and fed 5,000 men and a large number of women and children. Jesus loved to use mealtimes to teach and tell stories. Jesus celebrated and enjoyed feasts.

In the same way, my family often shares food with many different kinds of people. We don't like to see anyone leave the table hungry, so we always try to fix plenty with some left over. We may not be able to take five loaves and feed a multitude, but we share what we have with the poor and needy. We also love to tell stories just like Jesus did. Celebrations always involve good food and lots of stories. Our children and grandchildren learn from these stories. They sit at a formal table laden with food and hear how my Nannie taught school without pay for three years during the Great Depression. They hear about her efforts to feed hungry children in her community by pooling donated vegetables to make schoolhouse soup. As the children listen

and chuckle over the familiar stories, the stories become a part of them. The grandchildren never met Nannie, yet through her stories they have learned compassion and ingenuity. They have learned to value education and hard work. The stories and the lessons we impart become a part of the grandchildren's makeup, their heritage. Even though they never laid eyes on Nannie, her stories, not lectures, are what is remembered when we leave the table.

When Jesus fed people, they felt loved. When he told stories, lives were changed, and people learned about forgiveness. Gathering around Mama's, Nannie's, Gramps's, or Granny's tables made me feel loved. We shared not only food but also stories about the family and memories of past occasions. I think sharing food and stories helps heal the body, mind, and spirit. Sharing food and stories helps ease family problems and helps us to remember good times.

Jesus reached out his arms to gather people to him just as my family has done around the table with mealtimes. Like Christ, my family has strived to be inclusive instead of exclusive with our love and storytelling. I view sharing a meal with family and others as a vehicle to include them in an unparalleled fashion. Food can be the "circle that took him in." I see this in my business as well as in my family meals. I have seen intimacy established and hurts "made all better" with a lunch shared at one of my sewing seminars. Eating a meal with someone makes it possible to share a bit from your soul. I have seen how eating a meal in a business setting has led to better relationships with colleagues.

When on a mission journey, I saw the joy of Jesus evidenced in Brazilian church members who cooked delicious meals for our American mission team. They had been cooking all day to refresh us in the evening and served the meal with such love and joy. We did not even speak the same language, but the love expressed through the language of serving and sharing food is universal.

I have witnessed the pain of poverty as Jamaican ladies did not even have food to bring for lunch during a day of sewing and embroidery classes. We had sack lunches, but we chose to give them to the children. As teachers, we worked and praised the Lord all day with no food, just like our Jamaican students. This was one of very few days in my life that I have not had lunch.

I have grieved while working in villages in Africa, realizing that the people had no food or very little in the way of nutritious meals. I cried as I was presented with a live chicken after we had worked in medical/dental clinics all day in a remote village of Africa. I felt a bit awkward standing there holding the gift of a live chicken; however, I realized that this chicken was the only meat that the whole village would have had to cook. They had given me their best food. Food is a gift that is meant to be shared.

Suzanne and I now present our stories alongside our recipes and specially chosen scriptures to encourage you. I am grateful to our cooking family members who cooked and shared love with so many people. I pray that I might do half as good a job as they did.

A NOTE FROM MARTHA

Before I explain the journey of this book's creation, I would like to give you the three main purposes for writing it. First, I hope the scriptures and spiritual thoughts that Suzanne and I felt compelled to share will encourage you. Second, Suzanne and I have provided our favorite family recipes so they can become a cherished part of your recipe collection. And third, our intention was to present this as a how-to book, which not only encourages you to wax nostalgic about your own family stories that are centered around meals and cooking but to actually record them. We want to inspire your journey of writing a cooking memoir for your family. A compilation of family recipes is a priceless family treasure that can be given to children and grandchildren, and when you add your own stories and memories, it becomes the absolute easiest way to record part of your family heritage. We believe that memoir writing is one of the greatest gifts a person can give to his or her family—this generation and future ones as well. It is fun to write recipe memoirs because most of the work is already done and because food memories are usually such happy ones.

For years I have been telling my sewing students in person and through my weekly e-mail newsletters to write memoirs. I have said over and over, "If you don't write down your family stories, they will be gone forever. Do this for your children, your grandchildren, and for generations to come in the next century." And yet, when I sat down to write my own memoirs, I had no clue where to begin. I have authored more than fifty-five books in the sewing arena with my name prominently on the front cover, and I was at a complete loss as to where to start with my own life. Admittedly, I had lots of staff help with many of my sewing books in terms of sewing instruction and directions, but I had no one to turn to for help with the personal task that loomed before me. With that being said, I have always written antique descriptions, shared personal histories, and the stories. I have written a Dear Friends page in *Sew Beautiful* magazine for more than twenty years, and I write a free sewing newsletter every week with lots of family stories contained therein. This newsletter goes to more than 45,000 people, and I get more feedback about my stories than anything else. Basically, I have earned my living as a writer. And yet, here I sat, completely stumped by the idea of memoir writing.

Why do I tell you this? Because even though I am a professional writer and a former English teacher, I was truly challenged by the idea of writing my own memoirs. My questions were some of the same ones anyone would have: "Where on earth do I begin? Do I write about my childhood, my mother and daddy, my school experiences, my children when they were children, my career, my opening the business and growing it for nearly thirty years, my sewing/teaching stories, my grandparents, my spiritual journey, my husband, or my grandchildren? And once I pick one or some of these angles, where do I begin? Before I penned a single word, I think I purchased every book on memoir writing offered at Amazon.com. And still, nothing. In my mind, I could fill 100,000 pages with the memoirs of my family and still not cover everything. Where should I begin? That question weighed so heavily on my mind that I did nothing.

Fortunately, I have always loved to cook. My mother and grandmother loved to cook and cooked a lot throughout their lives. Both were school teachers as well. My sister, a social worker,

has always been a superb cook. My husband Joe's mother was an excellent cook and prepared a major meal at least once a day for virtually her entire adult life, (she lived to be eighty-five years old). My father was an excellent cook and actually taught my mother how to cook after they were married. He was a widower with three children and was in the food/coffee business.

Tucked away in my kitchen among my many, many cookbooks were those that belonged to Mama, Nannie (my grandmother), and Joe's mother. On the shelf alongside the cookbooks sat several recipe boxes; some were my Mama's, others are mine. Mama, Nannie, Joe's mother, and I saved handwritten recipes. We made notes in our cookbooks and added our own recipes to the pages wherever there was a blank space to write. We collected recipes given to all of us by our friends. I have recipes from Joe's aunts and my sister, and even recipes from my friends who live as far away as Australia.

I began to pray about my desire to leave a legacy of memoir for my family, which is rather large when you include my sewing family. Enter my daughter-in-law, Suzanne Crocker. Suzanne grew up in a missionary family in Guatemala, and her father is a Baptist preacher/missionary— and she is a fabulous cook. When Joe and I visited them in Africa, I was astounded at what she cooked with none of the conveniences and very few of the store-bought ingredients we have readily available in the United States. And she cooked three delicious meals a day! There are no McDonald's or Chick-fil-As in Africa. Quite the contrary; about once every six months, Suzanne, John, and the children would drive seven hours to a grocery store in Lome, purchase what they could on a missionary's salary, and transport the food back to Kara. Talk about planning one's meals! Once they returned to the States and I had the opportunity to visit and share meals on a more regular basis with Suzanne, I consulted with Suzanne and she happily agreed to co-author this book with me. With her knowledge, help, and encouragement, I pulled out of my writer's block and set to work.

Suzanne and I want to thank you for letting us share our family recipes and other important thoughts with you. We pray you will be blessed by this book, enjoy the delicious recipes, and share them with your family. Let us know which ones you like best!

". . . For I know the plans I have for you," says the Lord, "They are plans for good and not for disaster, to give you a future and a hope. In those days when you pray, I will listen to you. If you look for me wholeheartedly, you will find me."

—JEREMIAH 29:11–13

A NOTE FROM SUZANNE

I am an unabashed bookworm. I have always loved to read. When I was in middle school my dad was the pastor of a church in a rural farm community. Warwick had a population of 515 people, and there was only one girl my age in the entire town. Summers were long and hot. We weren't allowed to watch much TV, so for entertainment we rode our bikes up and down the dusty roads, built tree houses, and read books. I read everything I could get my hands on. Our town had a tiny library that was only open for a couple of hours twice a week. Every time the doors opened I was on the doorstep checking out another slew of books. Unfortunately, the library consisted of a single room in the city hall lined with bookshelves. It didn't take many years for me to read my way through all the fiction, so I started on the nonfiction. One summer I read all the encyclopedias (I know, my daughter already affectionately told me, "I hate to tell you this, Mom, but I think you may have been a nerd!"). Then I discovered the cookbooks. I already liked to cook, but this was different. There were exotic recipes from faraway places I had never visited—Poland, Russia, Thailand, and so forth. There were magical combinations of ingredients we already had in our home that made meals so different they tantalized your taste buds. Some of the cookbooks had stories, tips, and techniques. They really made fascinating reading for a bored little girl in a small town.

I was already surrounded by women who cooked. My mother always cooked wonderful meals from scratch. There wasn't any Hamburger Helper at our house! I had two grandmothers who cooked, and then there was my Aunt Peggy. She lived in the big city of Jacksonville, Florida.

Most of our vacations were spent at her house, and could that woman cook! In fact, she was such an incredible cook that she eventually catered my wedding. Whenever we arrived at her house she would have fabulous meals ready for us. She made dishes that we never made in our small town—lasagna, frippies, salads, chocolate chip cookies, etc. I know, that doesn't sound very exotic now, but thirty years ago if you came from a remote rural area, lasagna was very exotic!

As I became a young adult I collected recipes the way some people collect baseball cards. One of my most treasured wedding gifts was a set of handwritten cards from Aunt Peggy with many of her recipes. Little did I know that she would die when I was a young wife and that I wouldn't be able to call her and get more recipes anytime I wanted. Those recipes are tangible reminders of her love. Preparing them brings back happy memories of our times together. Seeing her handwriting on the cards and tasting those recipes that are so uniquely hers always makes me smile. Every year I make Cream Cheese Crescents for John, and every Christmas he comes into the kitchen, bites into one, and says, "Do you remember when your Aunt Peggy . . . ?"

Preparing good food is so much more than a chore. It is a gift and a privilege. The food you prepare nourishes your family, sets the stage for pleasant evening conversations, and knits you together. Years from now, your grown child will put something in his or her mouth and the taste will remind him or her of home and bring back memories of time spent together. It can be your ministry as you feed your family and others.

We want to do much more with this book than just share wonderful recipes. We want to encourage you to feed your family well, care for them, and build memories together. To that end, we have given you some really good recipes that are relatively easy to make. We want to encourage you and help you grow spiritually while you cook, so we have included some devotionals related to food; among our written memories are scriptures, and we have suggested ways to practically apply these teachings to your life. Lastly, we've tied many of our stories to our recipes, illustrating how cherished family memories can develop around meals, food, and cooking. If you don't have your own recipe file, you need to start one. Write down your stories together with your recipes and share them with your family. They will treasure this heartfelt gift for years to come.

HOW TO USE THIS BOOK

*Most cookbooks include just recipes. Most memoir books focus on life stories.
Most devotional books are filled with Bible verses. So why put them all together?
Writing my memoirs was one of my life's goals. Had I done it? Not yet.
Writing a devotional book was another goal of mine. Had I started it? No.
I also set a life goal of compiling my family recipes to pass down to future
generations. I was procrastinating on that one, too.*

When my daughters-in-law, particularly Suzanne, started asking me for copies of my recipes, I serendipitously came upon a relatively easy and enjoyable way to achieve all three goals. I discovered that when I wrote down each family recipe, I was compelled to write down any memory or family story surrounding the dish. Since mine is a Southern, Christian family, I found that not only were many of my life stories centered around food, but they also reflected Christian principles. It was just a natural progression to include favorite verses and events from the Bible. Suddenly the three projects I thought presented a monumental task were actually quite easy, and I have to admit, it was fun walking down a very tasty memory lane.

Suzanne and I want you to have the same amazing experience when you think about the special memories surrounding *your* family recipes, and we feel that it's so important to preserve those recipes and the stories behind them for future generations. We know that it can be hard to just sit down and start writing, so throughout the book we've included some tips to get you started. First, at the end of each chapter, you'll find stories from Suzanne and I that talk about our experiences with food and the memories attached to those dishes. At the end of these stories, we've included writing prompts that will help you start thinking about your own personal stories and family memories. Then, at the end of the book, you'll find our "Tell Your Own Story" appendix where we've provided space for you to begin writing down the recipes that have played a role in your life along with the memories that go along with them.

So get ready to do some Southern cooking, hear our stories, and tell your own as you begin your own personal walk down memory lane! Enjoy!

CHAPTER 1

Breads & Muffins

Jesus answered, "It is written: 'Man does not live on bread alone, but on every word that comes from the mouth of God.'"

—MATTHEW 4:4

Suzanne's Yeast Bread Making Tips

I learned bread making the hard way—by trial and error. John's first pastorate was in a rural community. We lived a long way from the grocery store, and I was home alone with the girls a lot. I grew a garden, canned a lot of our food, and baked most of our bread. Some of my initial efforts at bread making were less than successful. I wanted to include these tips at the beginning of the bread section so you won't have to learn by making the same mistakes that I did. Here are a few things I learned to help your yeast breads succeed:

1. Yeast is a living creature and has to be treated with care. You get the rising action of yeast as it eats a starch like sugar and produces air bubbles. If it gets too hot, you'll kill it, and your bread won't rise at all. Too cold and it will produce bubbles slowly and your bread will be pretty flat. The temperature should feel warm to you, but not so hot that you couldn't submerge your hand in it.

2. Yeast does not like metal. As much as possible use glass bowls and wooden spoons. Try not to have your yeast come into any prolonged contact with metal until it is in its final rising period.

3. Bread dough has doubled when you press two fingers into the dough and the dough does not spring back.

4. There is a major difference between bread flour and ordinary flour—bread flour is well worth the extra expense.

5. Kneading bread dough is hard work, but it gives your arms a better workout than the gym!

6. Do not let your dough dry out or form a crust before baking. Either cover it with plastic wrap sprayed with cooking spray or a warm moist towel.

Mama's Poppy Seed Bread

*Mama's Poppy Seed Bread did not last very long after it came out of the oven.
She frequently took a loaf to someone who was sick, and you cannot imagine what
joy it brought to have a hot loaf of delicious bread. She usually used two loaf pans,
one for us and one she would take to someone in need. Mama took missions of
mercy in the form of food to nearly everyone who was sick. That was just what she did.
When someone was really ill, she went home after teaching school all day and began
cooking various things. If the person had no one to fix a nutritious meal,
she usually cooked a big pot of soup and made some cornbread. If someone had
at least a meal prepared, Mama would take something very special like
poppy seed bread. Her generosity was always appreciated.*

—Martha—

BREAD		GLAZE
3 cups plain flour	1½ cups milk	¾ cup sugar
2 cups sugar	½ cup cooking oil	¼ cup orange juice
1½ teaspoons salt	1½ teaspoons vanilla	½ teaspoon vanilla
1½ tablespoons baking powder	1½ teaspoons butter flavoring	½ teaspoon almond
3 eggs	1½ teaspoons almond flavoring	½ teaspoon butter flavoring
	1½ tablespoons poppy seeds	

1. Preheat oven to 325°F.
2. Mix together all bread ingredients. Grease and flour two loaf pans or one bundt pan. Pour batter into prepared pan(s) and bake for 1 hour, then remove from oven and cool for 10 minutes.
3. While bread is cooling, mix together all glaze ingredients in a saucepan and heat to boiling. Remove from heat and immediately pour over bread.

Streusel Coffee Cake

I have been making this coffee cake since I was a teenager. When I first got married, it was the one breakfast that I knew how to cook well, and I cooked it often. Even today it is one of my kids' favorites for special occasions. It is also really good for carrying to brunches.

—Suzanne—

2½ cups self-rising flour

1½ cups sugar

2 eggs

1 cup milk

½ cup oil

1½ teaspoons vanilla

¾ cup packed brown sugar

3 tablespoons flour

1½ tablespoons cinnamon

½ stick butter

1. Preheat oven to 375°F. Put flour and sugar in a mixing bowl. In a smaller bowl, whisk eggs, milk, oil, and vanilla. Add to dry mixture all at once; stir to combine. Pour into a greased 9" x 13" glass pan.
2. In a separate bowl, mix brown sugar, flour, cinnamon, and butter until the mix is crumbly. Sprinkle over entire coffee cake. Bake for 30 minutes.

The Sovereign LORD is my strength! He makes me as surefooted as a deer, able to tread upon the heights.

—HABAKKUK 3:19

Yogurt Biscuits

My family eats a lot of biscuits, and I do mean a lot! I like variety and have several biscuit recipes that I use. This is probably the most unusual biscuit recipe, but it is delicious. These always come out really moist and flaky. This recipe was originally a recipe from Togo that developed from not having access to buttermilk.

—Suzanne—

2¼ cups self-rising flour

½ cup shortening

1 cup plain yogurt

1. Preheat oven to 425°F. In a medium bowl, add the flour and shortening, and mix using your fingers until pea-sized particles are formed (a process known as "cutting in").
2. Add yogurt, then stir just enough to make into dough (too much handling results in tough biscuits). Roll out dough and cut out biscuits in whatever size you like best. Bake for 8–10 minutes on ungreased cookie sheet.

Joyful is the person who finds wisdom, the one who gains understanding. For wisdom is more profitable than silver, and her wages are better than gold.

—PROVERBS 3:13–14

Blueberry Oat Bran Muffins

I must have made this recipe a thousand times. Twenty-five years ago, Joe and I discovered the health merits of oat bran. Joe, at that time, needed to lower his cholesterol. No longer eating eggs, bacon, and sausage in the mornings probably did more for lowering his cholesterol than the muffins. However, we have eaten these muffins nearly every morning since I started making them. We have hot muffins the first day, and I store the rest in the refrigerator. Each morning we take out two muffins, split them into three slices, spray with squirt butter, and toast in the oven. Along with some Greek yogurt, this is our breakfast. We set up our table with the muffins, sugar-free jelly or sugar-free syrup (Joe likes syrup better), and Greek yogurt. I read aloud from the Bible, and we discuss what we just read over breakfast.

—Martha—

1 16-ounce box oat bran such as Quaker Oats

2 bananas

1 cup skim milk (or other milk)

2 teaspoons baking powder

½ cup Egg Beaters (or eggs)

1 cup Splenda

Nuts (optional)

2 cup frozen blueberries

1. Preheat oven to 375°F. Combine all ingredients in a large bowl. This mixture looks like a hard lump when the frozen blueberries are added. Don't worry; that is what it is supposed to look like.
2. Spray muffin pan (12 muffins) with nonstick cooking spray. Spoon batter into muffin cups. Bake for 20–22 minutes.

Lemon Poppy Seed Mini Muffins

*These are a wonderful treat to serve when you have company. They are elegant,
but easy. That's a winning combination in my book.*

—Suzanne—

2 cups self-rising flour

¾ cup sugar

1 cup sour cream

½ cup vegetable oil

2 eggs

2 tablespoons poppy seeds

2 tablespoons milk

½ teaspoon vanilla extract

½ teaspoon lemon extract

1. Preheat oven to 400°F. In a large bowl, combine flour and sugar. Mix remaining ingredients
in a separate bowl.
2. Add wet ingredients to the dry ones all at once. Mix until just moistened.
Spoon into greased mini muffin cups and bake for 8–10 minutes.

Lemon Poppy Seed Mini Muffins

World's Best Banana Muffins

One thing we had in Togo was bananas—lots and lots of bananas. They were available all year round and never seemed to be out of season. Once or twice a week a lady would come to my house with a huge tray of bananas carefully balanced on her head. She probably carried about twenty-five pounds of bananas artistically arranged on her tray. I would select my bananas and pay her for them. She would then continue her stroll around town. Usually she sold her bananas three for a nickel. We always found ourselves with overripe bananas, caused by the heat. We had banana everything recipes, but this muffin recipe was by far our favorite. The kids never tired of these sweet muffins.

—Suzanne—

1¾ cups flour

1¼ teaspoons cream of tartar

½ teaspoon salt

¾ teaspoon baking soda

¾ cup sugar

2 beaten eggs

2 large or 3 small ripe bananas, mashed

½ cup oil

1. Preheat oven to 400°F. Mix together dry ingredients. Make a well in them, and add eggs, bananas, and oil. Stir until moistened; don't over mix.
2. Spoon batter into greased muffin tins, and bake for 18 minutes or until golden brown.

Sunshine Muffins

These are a citrusy treat perfect for a summer morning! Brenda Hearn was a missionary in the capital city of Lome. She was a very petite woman proving wrong the story that most good cooks are "robust." She made these muffins for us when we visited her in the capital.

—Suzanne—

1½ cups all-purpose flour

1 cup whole-wheat flour

1²/₃ cups sugar

2 teaspoons baking powder

½ teaspoon salt

½ cup coconut

½ cup chopped nuts

¾ cup melted butter

3 eggs, beaten

²/₃ cup orange juice

1 teaspoon vanilla extract

4 tablespoons orange marmalade

1. Preheat oven to 350°F. In a large bowl, mix flours, sugar, baking powder, salt, coconut, and nuts.
2. In separate bowl, mix remaining ingredients. Make a well in dry ingredients, add wet ingredients, and mix. Fill greased muffin cups. Bake for 15–20 minutes.

Apricot-Oatmeal Muffins

I have "1973" written on this recipe card. The boys and I were living in Gainesville, Florida. I was writing curriculum for Project FAIS at the P. K. Yonge Laboratory School of the University of Florida. My boys always loved muffins, and I was always trying to come up with something that they would eat for breakfast. I would make a pan, refrigerate the leftovers, and then toast them for breakfast for several days.

—Martha—

1 egg

1 cup buttermilk

½ cup brown sugar, firmly packed

⅓ cup vegetable shortening

1 cup sifted flour

1 teaspoon baking powder

1 teaspoon salt

½ teaspoon baking soda

1 cup old-fashioned oats, uncooked

½ cup dried apricots, finely chopped

1. Preheat oven to 400°F. Grease 12 muffin cups. Beat together egg, buttermilk, brown sugar, and shortening. In a separate bowl, sift together flour, baking powder, salt, and baking soda.
2. Add dry mixture, oats, and apricots to egg mixture. Stir only until dry ingredients are moistened. Fill muffin cups two-thirds full, and bake for 20–25 minutes until lightly browned.

Instant Lemon Muffins

Sweet enough for dessert, these muffins would also be a big breakfast treat.
You can easily carry them to church or any other potluck. I have always been a big fan
of muffins. They are easy to put in the freezer and just take out what you need.
When I was a little girl, Mama had a muffin pan. Although she did not use it
very often, it seemed that when she made muffins they were very special.

—Martha—

2 cups self-rising flour

1 3½-ounce box instant lemon pudding and pie filling

2 tablespoons sugar

¼ cup oil

⅓ cup milk

¼ cup confectioners' sugar to dust the tops of the cooked muffins

1. Preheat oven to 425°F. In a medium bowl, stir together flour, pudding, and sugar. In a separate small bowl, combine oil and milk. Add liquid ingredients to flour mixture, and stir only until flour is moistened.
2. Fill greased muffin cups ⅔ full, and bake for 20–25 minutes. Remove from pan and sprinkle with confectioners' sugar.

Whenever I pray, I make my requests for all of you with joy.

—PHILIPPIANS 1:4

Apple Nut Muffins

Apples were a sign that the economy of Togo was improving. Togo did not have the climate to grow apples, so they were an import. For several years we didn't see apples at all, and then they began to appear in expensive European grocery stores. Gradually they became more common, and by the time we left Togo they were commonly sold everywhere. They were still such a valuable commodity in my mind that it was hard to chop them up in a muffin unless we were really craving these!

—Suzanne—

1 egg

⅔ cup milk

½ cup oil

1 teaspoon vanilla

2 cups plain flour

¼ cup sugar

¼ cup brown sugar

1 tablespoon baking powder

½ teaspoon salt

½ cup nuts

1 chopped apple

1. Preheat oven to 400°F. Mix egg, milk, oil, and vanilla in a small bowl. Mix flour, sugar, brown sugar, baking powder, salt, nuts, and apple in another bowl.
2. Make a well in the dry ingredients, and pour wet ingredients in the middle. Stir until just moistened. Bake in a greased muffin pan for 12–15 minutes.

Breakfast Cups

My boys loved these for breakfast.
I fixed them often to rave reviews.
The entire dozen I would prepare would
be devoured by the four boys before
they left for school.

—Martha—

Nonstick cooking spray

1 can refrigerator biscuits

1 dozen eggs

1 pound sausage, browned and crumbled

1 7-ounce package shredded Cheddar cheese

1. Preheat oven to 350°F. Spray muffin cups with nonstick cooking spray. Flatten out the canned biscuits and press around the outside edges and bottom of each muffin cup to form a little biscuit cup.

2. Break 1 egg into each biscuit cup. Sprinkle sausage on the egg. Top with as much cheese as you like. Bake for about 15 minutes or longer depending on how done you like your eggs.

Baked Oatmeal

This is a quick and easy meal for a cold
winter morning. Even if you are not an
oatmeal fan, you'll enjoy this!
Sometimes I look for interesting ways to
"change" our usual breakfast items.
I don't remember where I first saw baked
oatmeal but it almost looked like cake
and I thought I might like to try it.

—Suzanne—

¾ cup sugar

1 stick melted butter

½ cup milk

2 eggs, beaten

1 teaspoon salt

1 teaspoon cinnamon

2 teaspoons baking powder

3 cups oatmeal, uncooked

Preheat oven to 350°F. In a large bowl, combine all ingredients and mix well. Bake in a greased 9" x 13" pan for 30–45 minutes or until golden brown. Serve hot with warm milk.

Oven-Baked Pancake Breakfast Coffee Cake

Oven-Baked Pancake Breakfast Coffee Cake

Everyone needs a few recipes they can make without a recipe card. This has ended up being one of those make-from-memory recipes that my family enjoys. I was initially given this recipe on a family mission trip to Arkansas. We were working to build a Christian camp. My job was to "chink" the log cabins and make them weatherproof. I spent hours perched on the scaffolding carefully caulking the cracks between the logs while John worried about me falling off (the men were doing heavier work like laying hardwood floors). It was an incredible time of ministry and fun working together, and the lady of the camp made it even better by fixing delicious meals for us like this oven-baked pancake.

—Suzanne—

2 cups powdered pancake mix

1 stick butter

½ cup brown sugar

1 cup syrup

1. Preheat oven to 375°F. Mix the pancake mix with water according to directions on box.
2. In a saucepan, mix butter, sugar, and syrup, then bring to a boil. Once it boils, pour the syrup mixture in the bottom of a greased 9" x 13" pan. Pour pancake mix on top. Bake for 30 minutes.

I have hidden your word in my heart, that I might not sin against you.

—PSALM 119:11

French Toast Bake

John's grandfather loved a big breakfast. He was from southern Alabama, and they know how to do a big country breakfast there. Christmas 2008 we decided to have a really big brunch Christmas morning (instead of a turkey lunch at my house) followed by a big turkey dinner at Mom Pullen's. Pa Pa absolutely loved it. We cooked all his favorites—country ham and biscuits, sausage gravy and biscuits, eggs, grits, fruit salad, and I don't know what all else. One of our new dishes to try was this French Toast Bake. It simplified things because you could make it the night before. Little did we imagine as we were enjoying all of our good food and fellowship that it would be the last Christmas that Pa Pa was able to get out and join us. Build memories while you can, because no one knows what tomorrow holds!

—Suzanne—

12 1"-thick slices day-old French bread

5 eggs, beaten

1 cup brown sugar, divided

2 teaspoons vanilla

½ teaspoon nutmeg

1 cup chopped pecans

¼ cup melted margarine or butter

2 cups fresh or frozen blueberries

Whipped cream for garnish (optional)

grated nutmeg for garnish (optional)

1. Place bread slices in the bottom of a greased 9" x 13" pan. In a large bowl, mix eggs, ¾ cup brown sugar, vanilla, and nutmeg. Pour mixture over the bread. Cover and put in refrigerator overnight.
2. Take pan out of refrigerator, and sprinkle with pecans; let set 30 minutes before baking.
3. Preheat oven to 400°F. Combine the melted butter and ¼ cup brown sugar. Drizzle over the top of the bread, and then bake for 25 minutes. Top with blueberries and bake for another 10 minutes. Before serving, garnish with whipped cream and nutmeg if so desired.

French Toast Bake

Sausage Cream Cheese Frippies

*We spent most vacations at Aunt Peggy's house. She could cook anything!
She usually cooked ahead of time so that she could spend time with us. We did all
the fun Florida things with Aunt Peg. We would visit the beach, do water slides, go
camping, and so forth. One time we even visited Disney World. Through all the fun,
Aunt Peg would go to her freezer and steadily pull out these wonderful meals she had
cooked ahead of time so that we could enjoy our time together. This recipe was one of
my favorite breakfasts, and it freezes well.*

—Suzanne—

1 pound ground chuck, browned

½ pound sausage, browned

8 ounces cream cheese

4 small cans refrigerator biscuits

1 cup mozzarella cheese

1. Mix ground chuck, sausage, and cream cheese. Refrigerate overnight to blend flavors.
2. Preheat oven to 400°F. Cut each biscuit in half and roll out really flat. Fill with mixture, top with mozzarella, and roll up. Place on greased cookie sheet. Bake for 15 minutes.

Devote yourselves to prayer with an alert mind and thankful heart.

—COLOSSIANS 4:2

Basic Cornbread

My in-laws always carry on about my cornbread. I love to serve it with hot soups and stews. It is so quick and easy to make. The secret to making it really good is to put several tablespoons of oil in a heavy cast-iron skillet and put it in a really hot (450°F) oven while you stir up the batter. When you pour the mixture into the hot oil, it starts to cook immediately and makes a really crisp crust.

—Suzanne—

½ cup oil, divided

1 cup self-rising cornmeal

1 cup self-rising flour

2 tablespoons brown sugar

½ cup dry powdered milk

2 eggs

1 cup milk

1. Preheat oven to 450°F. Put ¼ cup oil in a cast-iron skillet and put it in the oven while the oven preheats.
2. In a medium bowl, mix cornmeal, flour, brown sugar, and powdered milk. In separate bowl, stir eggs and milk together.
3. Combine wet and dry all at once and stir well. Immediately pour into hot skillet and return to oven. Bake for 15–25 minutes.

Mexican Cornbread

Cornbread by itself is a treat, but this cheesy cornbread full of good stuff is really a meal in itself. You'll enjoy the spice of the peppers combined with the creaminess of the cheese. Of all the breads that I make, I think this is Joe's favorite. Now, it is certainly not low calorie, but it is delicious. Joe especially likes this cornbread when I make vegetable soup or beef stew. The next day he crumbles leftover cornbread in a glass of buttermilk. By the way, cornbread in buttermilk eaten with a spoon is a great Southern favorite for those who like buttermilk.

—Martha—

2 eggs

½ cup salad oil

1 15-ounce can creamed corn

1 cup sour cream

1¾ cups self-rising corn meal

1 4-ounce can chili peppers

1 cup grated Cheddar cheese

Preheat oven to 350°F. Mix together all ingredients, except cheese, and pour half of the batter into a greased 9" x 13" pan. Sprinkle half of the cheese over mixture. Pour remaining batter on top, and top with the remaining half of the cheese. Bake for 45–60 minutes.

Joyful are people of integrity, who follow the instructions of the Lord.

—PSALM 119:1

Broccoli Cheese Cornbread

In the South we love cornbread. Most of my Nannie's meals included either homemade biscuits or homemade cornbread. There was plenty of butter and homemade jelly to go with both. Nannie always had homemade orange marmalade plus the usual assortment of fruit jellies she made during the summer and stored for the winter on wooden shelves in her cellar. To tell you the truth I have served this broccoli cornbread with just a glass of milk for a quick dinner for Joe and me. It looks to me like a balanced meal, and it is so good!

—Martha—

10 ounces frozen chopped broccoli

8 ounces grated sharp Cheddar cheese

4 eggs, beaten

1 Jiffy cornbread mix

1 stick margarine, melted

1. Preheat oven to 400°F. Add broccoli to a small saucepan of boiling water and cook until thawed, 2–3 minutes. Drain well.
2. Combine broccoli with the remaining ingredients, mix, and place in buttered 9" square dish and bake for 20–30 minutes.

Strawberry Bread

Strawberry Bread

This is actually another Aunt Peggy recipe. This moist sweet bread is perfect for brunches or any special breakfast occasion. My dear Aunt Peggy was a magnificent cook—truly magnificent. She could make "fancy" things as well as everyday dishes and they all tasted great. We always loved to go to her house to visit. I might add that we loved her meals. She was considered the best cook in our family.

—Suzanne—

3 cups flour

1 teaspoon salt

1 teaspoon baking soda

3 teaspoons cinnamon

3 eggs

2 cups sugar

1½ cups oil

2 10-ounce packs frozen whole strawberries (without syrup), defrosted

1. Preheat oven to 375°F. In a medium bowl, sift together flour, salt, baking soda, and cinnamon. In a separate small bowl, beat eggs.
2. Add eggs, sugar, oil, and strawberries to flour mixture. Mix well and pour into two greased loaf pans. Bake for 1 hour or until lightly browned and done in the center.

Remember your promise to me; it is my only hope. Your promise revives me; it comforts me in all my troubles.

—PSALM 119:49–50

Martha's Famous Angel Biscuits

We have many requests to repeat this recipe. Mama kept these in her freezer at all times. My son, John, loves these, and Suzanne makes them often. Anytime Camp and John spent the night or weekend with Mama she always had these ready for them. I think the boys used to eat a dozen or more apiece. Mama had strawberry jam (homemade) ready to serve with real butter on these biscuits, but they're also delicious with apple butter. I have made these instead of homemade rolls at family dinners. They are just as popular. In the early days of the School of Art Fashion, I would make dozens and dozens of these for the ladies when they came to our home. They always received rave reviews and still do whenever I bake them.

—Martha—

5 cups flour	1 teaspoon baking soda	1 package highly active dry yeast
¼ cup sugar	1 teaspoon salt	2 tablespoons warm water
1 tablespoon baking powder	1 cup butter	2 cups buttermilk

1. Preheat oven to 375°F. In a large bowl, mix together flour, sugar, baking power, baking soda, and salt. Add butter and combine until pea-sized particles are formed.

2. Dissolve yeast in warm water and add to buttermilk. Add mixture to dry ingredients and mix well.

3. Turn out onto lightly floured board. Roll out and cut. I use a biscuit cutter and make them in either small sizes or larger sizes depending on my mood. Bake on cookie sheet until very lightly browned, approximately 12–14 minutes. You can also put these biscuits in muffin tins so they come out of the oven looking like Parker House Rolls, which originated in a famous Boston hotel. For Christmas, I cut out large biscuits, dip them in butter, and fold them in half before placing in Teflon-coated muffin pans. Sometimes I just bake them flat like biscuits.

4. To freeze, place uncooked biscuits on cookie sheet and freeze. After they are frozen, store them in freezer bags. About one hour before baking, take them out and brush with melted butter. Bake until brown, approximately 12–14 minutes until brown.

Martha's Famous Angel Biscuits

Dr. Pepper Biscuits

This recipe is from an old cookbook that Mama always had in her kitchen. These biscuits are easy to make and good to eat with melted butter inside. If you have guests, Dr. Pepper biscuits are a good conversation starter. Who in the world ever heard of using Dr. Pepper to make biscuits? Frequently I make these and freeze them. When ready to cook, just thaw and pop them into the oven. When I serve spaghetti I love to have these biscuits ready to butter and enjoy. They are also good with soups and stews. Actually I think they are good with anything, but they are really not a breakfast biscuit but rather a lunch or dinner bread.

—Martha—

2 cups Bisquick mix
½ teaspoon dried Italian seasoning
⅔ cup Dr. Pepper

Preheat oven to 425°F. Mix Bisquick and dried Italian seasoning. Add Dr. Pepper, then work into a soft ball. Roll dough to ½" thickness and cut with a biscuit cutter. Bake for 10–12 minutes (suitable for freezing).

But the Holy Spirit produces this kind of fruit in our lives: love, joy, peace, patience, kindness, goodness, faithfulness, gentleness, and self-control. There is no law against these things!

—GALATIANS 5:22–23

My Favorite Pumpkin Bread

This recipe card is so stained that I had to work hard to decipher it. Every Thanksgiving we make a big batch of this and enjoy it for our Thanksgiving breakfast. We always make enough to share.

—Suzanne—

3½ cups flour

3 cups sugar

1 teaspoon cinnamon

2 teaspoons baking soda

4 eggs

1 cup oil

½ teaspoon baking powder

½ teaspoon nutmeg

½ teaspoon cloves

½ teaspoon salt

⅔ cup water

2 cups pumpkin

Preheat oven to 375°F. Mix all ingredients well. Pour into 3 greased loaf pans. Bake for 45 minutes.

Church Ladies' Quick Rolls

I was a teenager when this quick roll recipe came through our church. It was amazing how quickly you can make these light and fluffy rolls. Once the secret was out, everyone made these rolls. For a while they were a big treat that appeared at every church dinner.

—Suzanne—

1 cup sour cream

1 stick margarine

1¾ cups self-rising flour

1. Preheat oven to 400°F. Cream together sour cream and margarine. Add flour.
2. Place in ungreased muffin tins. Bake for 7 minutes. Serve hot. They are not nearly as good once they cool off.

Dressing

I love my grandmothers' dressing recipes. Both of my grandmothers made wonderful dressing, but their recipes tasted very different. This is one of those recipes that is impossible to measure because it really depends on how much you are making. I always make lots of soup and cornbread leading up to Thanksgiving and put the leftover cornbread and breakfast biscuits in the freezer to wait for dressing-making time.

—Suzanne—

8 cups cornbread

4 cups biscuits, crumbled

1 stick butter

1 onion, diced

2 stalks celery, diced

2 teaspoons crushed sage

1 teaspoon salt

½ teaspoon pepper

1 quart chicken or turkey broth

1. Preheat oven to 375°F. Crumble cornbread and biscuits in a big bowl.
2. In a pan over medium heat, melt the butter, then add the onions and celery, and cook until brown, about 5 minutes. Stir the sage, salt, pepper, and cooked onion and celery into the cornbread mixture. Pour broth into it and stir until whole mixture is wet. Bake for 45 minutes.
3. **Note:** Maw's version—Maw always added "stuff" to her dressing, and it was a very heavy, moist dressing. My favorite: Brown 1 pound sausage and add it along with the grease at the point when you are adding the onions to the mix. Beat four eggs and add to mix. Add enough broth to make it really, really wet. Then bake it as indicated above. She also made oyster dressing by leaving out the sausage and adding a can of oysters.

Cheddar and Chive Bread

This bread is so easy! And I have found that any kind of homemade bread makes a meal real memorable. Since this recipe uses a loaf of French bread, I can have "homemade," which really isn't homemade at all. Daddy loved to have a loaf of French bread, which was not really very Southern; however, Daddy lived in New York and New Jersey for twenty-five years as a young man. I thought this "recipe" was very elegant when I was a child. Notice we used dried chives. In the South, fresh herbs were not too well known.

—Martha—

1 loaf French bread
1 cup shredded Cheddar cheese
1 cup mayonnaise
¼ cup dried chives

1. Preheat oven to 325°F. Slice bread at 1" intervals, making sure to slice almost to the bottom crust but not all the way through.
2. Mix cheese, mayonnaise, and chives. Spread one side of each slice with the mixture, and wrap whole loaf in aluminum foil. Bake for about 15 minutes.

The faithful love of the Lord never ends! His mercies never cease. Great is his faithfulness; his mercies begin afresh each morning. I say to myself, "The Lord is my inheritance; therefore, I will hope in him!"

—LAMENTATIONS 3:22–25

Herbed Onion Bread

*Daddy was an excellent Italian cook. He made the world's best spaghetti.
Mama would always do the salad and the bread for our Italian meals. I think this
recipe is similar to one of the easy breads that Mama baked for us. Daddy lived in
New York City for twenty-five years before we moved back south. He loved
replicating the fabulous things he had learned in New York City, such as
"fancy French bread" concoctions. When I was a child in Scottsboro, Alabama,
I thought store-bought French bread was very fancy.*

——Martha——

1 loaf French bread

⅔ cup butter, softened

1 teaspoon basil

1 teaspoon lemon juice

2 teaspoons finely chopped onion

1 teaspoon chopped fresh parsley

Preheat oven to 250°F. Slice bread at about ¾" intervals, but don't slice all the way
through to the crust. Mix together remaining ingredients and spread in between the slices.
Heat on cookie sheet for 25 minutes.

My Daddy's Hushpuppies

*My daddy is the hushpuppy maker in our house. I don't know how many times
I have walked into the kitchen to find him slowly and deliberately chopping
his onion very fine and carefully dipping the batter into the hot oil.
None of the rest of us ever really mastered this process, and it was just
one more way he told us that he loved us.*

—Suzanne—

¾ cup self-rising cornmeal

2 tablespoons flour

¼ cup plain cornmeal

½ onion, finely diced

¼ teaspoon baking powder

½–1 cup milk

Oil for frying

1. Mix all dry ingredients. Stir in enough milk to make a very thick batter.
2. Pour ½" oil into a large skillet and heat to 350°F. Drop batter, by rounded tablespoonfuls, into hot oil and fry. Turn once to make sure both sides cook evenly.

*So, my dear brothers and sisters, be strong and immovable. Always work
enthusiastically for the Lord, for you know that nothing you do for
the Lord is ever useless.*

—1 CORINTHIANS 15:58

Amish Potato Rolls

This is a no-fail recipe. It is a good place to start making bread dough because the potatoes give the yeast extra starch. I've never had these fail.

—Suzanne—

3 packages active dry yeast	1 cup unseasoned, warm mashed potatoes	²⁄₃ cup shortening
1½ cups warm water		1½ teaspoons salt
2 eggs	²⁄₃ cup sugar	6–7 cups flour

1. Dissolve yeast in warm water in a large bowl. Stir in eggs, potatoes, sugar, shortening, salt, and 3 cups flour. Beat until smooth. By hand, stir in enough remaining flour to make a stiff dough.

2. Knead on floured counter for 5 minutes. Put in greased bowl and turn oiled side up. Cover bowl tightly and refrigerate at least 8 hours, but no longer than 5 days. From this point you can make any type of bread you desire:

3. Loaf bread: Preheat oven to 375°F. Divide the dough in half, and then divide each half in half again; shape into four loaves. Let rise until doubled, then bake two loaves at a time on a greased cookie sheet for about 20–30 minutes or until brown.

4. Cinnamon rolls: Preheat oven to 400°F. Roll a third to half of the dough into a large rectangle. Mix ½–1 cup sugar with 2–3 teaspoons cinnamon, and sprinkle ⅓ of the mixture over each ⅓ of the dough. Starting at long end, roll it up and press edge shut. Slice in 1"–2" wide slices and place on greased cookie sheet. Cover with wet towel and let rise until doubled in size. Bake for 10 minutes or until lightly browned.

5. Rolls: Preheat oven to 400°F. Roll to about ½" thick, cut into desired shape, and place on cookie sheet. Let double, then bake for 10 minutes.

6. **Doughnuts:** Roll dough to ½" thickness. Cut with doughnut cutter, cover with wet towel until doughnuts double in size, approximately 1–1½ hours depending on temperature of your dough. Fry one or two at a time in hot (350°F) oil. (I usually fry them in my cast-iron skillet because it keeps a more constant heat.) Dust with powdered sugar or vanilla glaze (for glaze, mix 1¾ cups powdered sugar, ¼ cup milk, and ½ teaspoon vanilla until smooth).

Mrs. Fehey's New Jersey Bread

When Mama married Daddy and moved to New Jersey, she could not cook anything. She adored her neighbors, and they graciously helped her learn to cook. Mrs. Fehey taught Mama to make bread, and Mama always had this recipe from Mrs. Fehey in her recipe box. My guess would be that it was written in 1942 since that is the year she moved to New Jersey. A little joke from Mama used to be that Mrs. Fehey helped her make thirty apple pies in one month, one each day, since Daddy loved apple pie, and Mama was determined to make it perfectly—puff pastry and all. Mama was always known for her yeast bread and rolls, and here is her bread recipe exactly as she wrote it in 1942.

—Martha—

1 yeast cake (use 1 package active dry yeast)	1½ cups milk	1 tablespoon salt
¼ cup warm water	2 tablespoons shortening	6–8 cups flour
	2 tablespoons sugar	1 cup cold water

1. Dissolve yeast in warm water and let stand 15 minutes. In a medium saucepan over medium-high heat, heat milk until bubbles start to form, then add shortening, sugar, and salt. Remove from heat, pour into large mixing bowl, then add 1 cup cold water.

2. When lukewarm, add yeast. Add 1 cup flour, beat, and add additional flour 1 cup at a time, beating after each cup, until too stiff to handle with spoon. Toss on floured bread board.

3. Knead flour until it no longer sticks to the board. Put in greased bowl, cover, and let rise 1½–2 hours.

4. Toss out on floured board again and cut in half. Knead each loaf and put in greased pans. Cut quick gash in each loaf and let rise for 1–2 hours.

5. As bread nears the end of the rising time, preheat oven to 400°F. Bake for 20 minutes, then reduce to 350°F and bake for 30 minutes.

Mama's Refrigerator Rolls

These are Mama's famous rolls she always baked for our sewing events as well as for our family. Mama would make them and put them in the freezer, bringing them out for any occasion. She cut out circles and folded a piece over in what she called Parker House Rolls, which originated in a famous hotel in Boston. She always brushed them with butter after bringing them out of the oven.

—Martha—

2 cups boiling water

½ cup plus ½ teaspoon sugar

1 tablespoon salt

2 tablespoons shortening

2 cakes quick-acting yeast (use 2 packages yeast)

¼ cup lukewarm water

2 beaten eggs

8 cups bread flour, sifted before measuring

1. In a large bowl, mix together boiling water, ½ cup sugar, salt, and shortening. Cool until lukewarm. Add yeast to ¼ cup lukewarm water and stir to combine; add ½ teaspoon sugar, and stir into first mix.

2. Add beaten eggs, stir in 4 cups flour, and beat well. Stir in 4 more cups flour. Put dough in a greased bowl, brush top of dough with melted butter, and seal tightly before putting in the refrigerator. Let sit in refrigerator for at least 8 hours and no longer than 5 five days.

3. Take dough out of the refrigerator, shape into rolls, place on greased cookie sheet, cover, and let rise for 1 hour. Preheat oven to 425°F while dough is rising. Bake for 15–20 minutes.

Easy Pizza Dough

When we were overseas, we almost always had homemade pizza on Friday nights.
Who wouldn't when you can enjoy it made on a homemade crust?
My mother-in-law would mail us bubble-wrapped packages filled with pepperoni
so we never ran out. After eating pizza and drinking cold Cokes in glass bottles,
we would either watch a video or play a game with the kids. Now that the girls
are older and rarely home on a Friday, I miss those times.

—Suzanne—

1 package dry yeast

1½ cups warm water

4 cups sifted flour

2 tablespoons oil

1 teaspoon salt

1. In a medium bowl, dissolve yeast in water. Add remaining ingredients and stir to combine.
2. Turn dough out onto a floured surface and knead for 10 minutes.
   Cover with damp cloth and let rise for about 2 hours.
3. Preheat oven to 425°F. Pat and stretch the dough to cover two large pizza pans.
   Spread on your favorite sauce and toppings. Bake for 15 minutes.

Sopapillas

One thing our family really enjoyed when the girls were younger was to have a restaurant night. Every so often we would pick a theme, like Chinese or Mexican, and let the girls spend the day helping me make special foods for the celebration. They would decorate the room in the theme and then color menus. By the time their dad came in from the village, the whole room would be transformed into a theme restaurant, and we would enjoy the special treats we had cooked together. Sopapillas are a lot of work to make, but the memories made while doing something like this with your preschooler are priceless.

—Suzanne—

4 cups flour	1 package active dry yeast	1½ cups milk
1½ teaspoons salt	1 tablespoon plus ¼ cup (for topping) sugar	2 teaspoons cinnamon
1 teaspoon baking powder		Oil for frying (you need about 2" of oil in pan)
1 tablespoon shortening	¼ cup warm water	

1. In a large bowl, combine flour, salt, and baking powder. Add shortening and combine until pea-sized particles are formed.

2. Dissolve yeast and 1 tablespoon sugar in warm water, being careful to use nonmetallic bowls and spoons. In a small saucepan over medium heat, heat milk until it starts to steam and small bubbles form, but do not bring to a boil. Remove from heat and let cool down. Add yeast mixture to cooled scalded milk.

3. Make a well in the dry ingredients, add the wet ones, and mix to combine. Turn dough out onto floured surface and knead 15–20 times; set dough aside to rest for 10 minutes. Roll to ¼" thickness or even thinner. Cut into 2" x 2" squares.

4. Preheat oil in heavy-bottomed pan to 420°F. Mix ¼ cup sugar and cinnamon. Fry sopapillas two at a time until lightly browned, approximately 30 seconds to 2 minutes. While hot, sprinkle with sugar and cinnamon mixture.

Brown-and-Serve Yeast Dinner Rolls

Homemade bread will definitely make dinner memorable. My family loves bread of any kind. These rolls are relatively easy to make and can be made ahead of time and frozen.

—Suzanne—

½ cup milk

2 packages active dry yeast

1 tablespoon plus ¼ cup sugar

1 cup warm water

2¼ teaspoons salt

¼ cup oil

4 cups flour

1. In a small saucepan over medium heat, heat milk until it starts to steam and small bubbles form, but do not bring to a boil. Remove from heat and let cool down.
2. Add yeast, 1 teaspoon sugar, and warm water to milk and mix. Set aside until yeast is dissolved and bubbly.
3. Mix together remaining sugar, salt, oil, and 2 cups flour. Beat really well, and then add 1–2 more cups of flour until it makes a stiff dough. Place in a well-greased bowl and flip over. Cover with plastic wrap or a warm, wet towel. Let rise for about 1 hour. Form rolls and put in greased muffin tins. Cover and let rise until doubled, approximately 1 hour depending on temperature of your dough.
4. Preheat oven to 275°F. Bake for 25 minutes; do not brown. Place in a single layer in containers to freeze. At serving time, bake at 400°F for 7–10 minutes until brown.

Easy French Bread

This bread is a good place to start if you don't have much experience making bread. It is a relatively easy recipe that never fails. It is really good with lasagna or spaghetti. When we were in Africa I had to make all of my bread from scratch. This was always a family favorite and was eaten very quickly after I made new loaves.

—Suzanne—

2 packages active dry yeast

1 teaspoon plus 2 tablespoons sugar

½ cup warm water

2 tablespoons shortening

2 teaspoons salt

2 cups boiling water

7–8 cups bread flour

1 egg, beaten

2 tablespoons poppy seeds

1. In a small bowl, dissolve yeast and 1 teaspoon sugar in the warm water. In another bowl, mix remaining sugar, shortening, salt, and boiling water. Let cool to lukewarm, then add yeast mixture. Stir in flour and turn out on a lightly floured bread board to knead for 10 minutes. Let rise for about 1 hour until doubled.

2. Cut in half and roll each half into a 12" x 15" rectangle. Roll the rectangle up and place on a greased cookie sheet. Cut slashes in top and cover. Let rise 45 minutes.

3. As bread nears the end of its rise, preheat oven to 400°F. Brush bread with beaten egg and sprinkle with poppy seeds. Bake for 20 minutes.

Little Braided Herb Breads

Someone decided to organize a progressive dinner for one of our first Christmases in Togo. We set up several different homes and designated who would cook what and in what order we would go around. I was in charge of breads and salads. This particular bread recipe originated from that party, and it was delicious. We had a big mix of Americans at our house, including missionaries of various denominations to World Health Organization pilots and mechanics who lived in Togo while working on various projects. It was great fun and kept homesickness at bay.

—Suzanne—

½ cup sugar	1 cup milk	¼ cup grated Parmesan and Romano cheese plus additional cheese for dusting
2 teaspoons salt	6 tablespoons margarine	
3 packages active dry yeast (or 3 tablespoons)	½ cup water	1½ teaspoons thyme
6–7 cups bread flour	3 large eggs	1 teaspoon Italian spice mix

1. Mix sugar, salt, yeast, and 2 cups flour in bowl. In a saucepan set to low, heat milk, margarine, and ½ cup water. After heating, let it cool until you can barely hold your hand on the bottom of the pot.

2. In a stand mixer or large bowl, combine the wet and dry mixtures and eggs, and mix on low for 2 minutes, then add cheese, thyme, and Italian spices. Beat 2 minutes longer. With wooden spoon, stir in 3 more cups flour.

3. Turn onto floured counter and knead for 10 minutes. Shape into ball and place in a greased bowl (turn once so greasy side is up), cover, and let rise about 1 hour. Cut dough into 9 pieces. Roll each piece into an 18" rope.

4. Take three ropes at a time and loosely braid them. Repeat three times. Cut each of these loaves in half and place in small greased loaf pan. You now have six small loaves. Brush tops with olive oil and sprinkle with small amount of cheese. Cover and let rise for about 30 minutes. While dough is rising, preheat oven to 400°F. Bake for 15 minutes or until golden.

Marsha's Loaf Bread

Marsha's family lived way out in the bush in Togo. They had lots of teams come out to help them, and Marsha was responsible for cooking for these teams. Store-bought bread was not an option, so she had to bake huge batches of bread. Once she multiplied this recipe and set bread dough out to rise in every conceivable container, including a pressure cooker. As it rose, the heat sealed the pressure cooker and Marsha couldn't get it open. She called her husband to help, and after his efforts and much maneuvering, the top flew off hitting Mike in the forehead and knocking him unconscious. Marsha thought she had killed him! Can you imagine death by bread baking? Mike turned out to be fine, and we all learned our lesson about never letting bread dough rise in a pressure cooker!

—Suzanne—

3 tablespoons yeast

4 cups warm water

2 tablespoons plus ¼ cup sugar

1 tablespoon salt

½ cup oil

8–10 cups bread flour

1. In small bowl, mix yeast, warm water, and 2 tablespoons sugar. In very large bowl, mix ¼ cup sugar, salt, oil, and 4 cups flour. Add the liquid mixture to flour mixture, and stir well. Add more flour, 2 cups at a time, until it is difficult to stir.

2. Turn onto counter and knead until smooth. Place in greased bowl and flip dough to grease it. Cover. Let rise until doubled.

3. Punch dough down, then divide and place in 4 greased loaf pans; let rise until doubled again, approximately 1 hour depending on the temperature of your dough. While dough is rising, preheat oven to 400°F. When dough has doubled, bake for 20–30 minutes.

GROCERIES IN A '57 CHEVY

—Martha—

[Dorcas] was always doing
kind things for others and helping the poor.

—ACTS 9:36

My grandmother was a great helper. She taught in the Alabama Public School system for forty-four years. A few years after she retired in 1954, she and my grandfather purchased a brand new turquoise 1957 Chevrolet automobile with a stick shift. The year I turned sixteen, they taught me how to drive in that very car. Nannie was always ready to help anyone with anything she could. She was sixty-two when she retired and became more aware that not many of her friends drove anymore.

She began her own personal ministry of driving all of the senior citizens to the grocery store and assisted them as they made their selections and put their groceries in the car. If they needed help once they returned home, she would stay and help unload their items. She continued this kindness until she was in her mid-eighties and could no longer see to drive. The old '57 Chevy just kept chugging and chugging along and was still in perfect condition long after she died. I once accompanied Nannie and one of her friends on their shopping excursion. I remember them discussing at length the cost per ounce of nearly every product they bought. Back then, there were

no little signs displayed under each item to provide shoppers with that information; my Nannie just figured it out in her head. She had an impressive mathematical mind. On that particular trip the two little old ladies spent quite a long time in the English pea section making sure they selected peas which were the very least expensive per ounce.

My grandmother was frugal, and it served her family well. She recorded every single expenditure she made. Her "books" were nothing fancy; they came from the dime store. But I still have them, and today they are part of my treasure of family heirlooms. She usually just recorded groceries as "groceries," but if she ran back to buy milk or bread, she listed those purchases individually as to their cost that day. She ran an efficient home and taught school, while my grandfather ran his two businesses; he was a farmer and a carpenter.

Helping the elderly with basic needs like shopping for groceries is one way we can be like Dorcas. It is hard to imagine not being able to even do something as basic as drive to the grocery store, but there are many people in that situation. Think about how you can help a shut-in whom you know.

Tell Your Story

1. Can you remember watching an adult in your life helping someone else when you were a child? What did they do? Did you participate? _____

_____

2. How did seeing them do these things affect you? What do you do differently now because of their actions? _____

_____

A WHOLE REFRIGERATOR FULL OF FOOD

—Martha—

Devote yourselves to prayer with an alert mind and a thankful heart.

—COLOSSIANS 4:2

Wealth is often in the eyes of the beholder. When I was in graduate school I lived in student housing with my two little boys, Camp and John. Our student housing consisted of an apartment at Northington Campus and was in pitiful shape. In fact, the apartments were going to be demolished as soon as the last students moved out. The Northington Campus Apartments were old army barracks left over from World War II. However, the rent was perfect, only $61 per month including utilities. These apartments were actually blown up in a Burt Reynolds movie shortly after we moved to Huntsville.

In spite of being a poor graduate student, I was able to make sure our family always had plenty to eat. It just was not very fancy, to be frank. We always had milk, bread, cheese, orange juice, Cream of Wheat, fresh fruit, peanut butter, jelly, Campbell's soup, green beans, Le Sueur peas, and potpies (10 for $1). I always had chicken and ground beef in the freezer, but you could not see that when you opened the tiny apartment-size refrigerator.

One day we went to Clanton to visit with my sister, Mary, and her husband, Alex, who had just graduated from law school. The boys were totally amazed at their apartment with carpeted floors. Mary had just started her job as a social worker. They had purchased a very small boat, which was on a trailer in the parking lot of their apartment. Camp and John were astounded to realize that Uncle Alex and Aunt Mary owned a real boat.

Later that evening, Camp came in the living room and announced "Mama, Aunt Mary and Uncle Alex are rich. They have a boat and a whole refrigerator full of food." Nearly forty years after that evening in Clanton, I realize that for many people a refrigerator of food would mean wealth. For many around the world even owning a refrigerator would be the ultimate luxury. Having enough food to eat is not a reality for so much of the world's population. Even looking back on the "poverty" of my student housing days, I realize that we had plenty of good, nutritious food. So many mothers in the world cannot say that.

Learning to have a thankful heart in whatever circumstances God places us in is the real key to wealth. Even a little can seem like a lot when it is received with thankfulness.

Tell Your Story

1. Write about a time when something that is common now seemed like a luxury. _____

_____

_____

_____

2. What is the most primitive living situation you have endured? What were you thankful for while living there? _____

_____

_____

CHAPTER 2

Soups, Salads,
&
Sides

*You cause grass to grow for the livestock and plants
for people to use. You allow them to produce food
from the earth.*

—PSALM 104:14

Black Bean Soup

A lot of Guatemalans eat black beans at every meal. For breakfast they are fried into patties, at other meals they are often served puréed over rice. Growing up in Guatemala, I loved black beans. When I first made this soup I was afraid my kids wouldn't like it, but they thoroughly enjoyed it! Even if you are not a black bean fan, you should give this recipe a try.

—Suzanne—

1 onion, diced

2 tablespoons garlic, chopped

2 carrots, finely chopped

3 tablespoons vegetable oil

2 15-ounce cans black beans

1 chicken bouillon cube

1 teaspoon chili powder

2 teaspoons cumin

Sour cream and green onions (optional)

1. In a saucepan over medium heat, lightly brown onion, garlic, and carrots in oil. Drain the beans and add to saucepan. Add 2 cans of water. Add bouillon cube, chili powder, and cumin, then simmer for 30 minutes. Take 1 cup of soup and purée in blender, then add back to saucepan. This will thicken your soup and give it a rich base.

2. Serve soup topped with a dollop of sour cream and a sprinkle of green onion slices.

Vegetable Minestrone Soup

This delicious recipe is from Frances Edge Hash, my childhood friend.
—Martha—

3 tablespoons olive oil

1 pound sweet or spicy sausage, casing removed and crumbled

1 large yellow onion, finely chopped

1 35-ounce can plum tomatoes, chopped

1 tablespoon salt

1 teaspoon black pepper

2 teaspoons sugar

2 tablespoons minced fresh basil (2 teaspoons dried)

1 large head Savoy cabbage, shredded

6 large carrots, diced

3 large celery ribs, diced

2½ quarts chicken broth

½ cup long-grain or Arborio rice

1 20-ounce can white cannelloni beans, drained

1 20-ounce can kidney beans, drained

Freshly grated or shredded Parmesan or Romano cheese

Chopped fresh parsley (optional)

1. In an 8-quart pot, heat olive oil over medium heat. Add sausage, turn to low heat, and sauté just until it loses its pinkness, about 2 or 3 minutes.

2. Add onion and sauté until soft but not brown. Add tomatoes, salt, pepper, sugar, and basil. Cook, uncovered, stirring frequently, for 15 minutes.

3. Add cabbage; cook and stir for 5 minutes. Add carrots and celery; cook and stir an additional 5 minutes.

4. Pour in chicken broth; bring to boil over high heat. As soon as soup reaches a boil, turn heat to low, cover pot, and simmer for 45 minutes, stirring frequently.

5. Stir in rice; cover pot and cook, undisturbed, for 10 minutes (if using brown rice, cook for about 30–40 minutes).

6. Stir in both cans of beans; cook covered for 5 minutes. Remove pot from heat and let soup rest for 2 hours, covered. If sausage is not lean, skim off any surface fat. Before serving, garnish with Parmesan or Romano cheese and fresh parsley if so desired.

Fear of the Lord is the foundation of true knowledge, but fools despise wisdom and discipline.—**PROVERBS 1:7**

Vegetable Minestrone Soup

Moldovan Cabbage and Tomato Soup

A couple of years ago we studied Moldova during our week of prayer. I was shocked to learn of the physical and spiritual poverty of this country in Europe. As one of the learning exercises, we made a Moldovan recipe. It was wonderful! I'm not a cabbage fan and didn't expect to enjoy it. This is an adaptation of this recipe, and it is delicious!

—Suzanne—

1 pound lean ground beef

½ cup chopped onion

½ head cabbage, finely chopped

1 28-ounce can diced tomatoes

1 15-ounce can tomato sauce

1 quart chicken broth

¼ cup vinegar

1 tablespoon paprika

Salt and pepper to taste

4 cups prepared rice

In a large saucepan over medium heat, brown ground beef and onion. Drain and add cabbage, tomatoes, tomato sauce, broth, vinegar, and paprika. Season with salt and pepper to taste. Simmer for 1 hour. Serve over rice.

Rejoice in our confident hope. Be patient in trouble, and keep on praying.

—ROMANS 12:12

Chicken Tortilla Soup

This rich, cheesy soup is incredibly good! Ben likes to eat it with corn chips, and the rest of us love it in a bread bowl. I usually cheat and make the bread bowls with half of a loaf of frozen bread dough defrosted and shaped into a round loaf. Then we cut the top out and fill it with soup. You cannot imagine how much John and Sarah Joy like fresh bread and soup. In fact, last night I made six loaves for four of us, and they were discussing who got the extra bread, plus they finished off mine!

—Suzanne—

1½ pounds boneless chicken breasts

16 ounces Velveeta cheese

1 14-ounce can tomatoes and green chilies

1 teaspoon cumin

1 10½-ounce can cream of chicken soup

1 10½-ounce can cream of mushroom soup

1 onion, chopped

1 bell pepper, chopped

1 tablespoon oil

1 12-ounce can evaporated milk

3 tablespoons cornstarch

1. Boil chicken in 6 cups of water for about 30 minutes to make a broth. Measure 4 cups chicken broth into soup pot and reserve chicken. Chop Velveeta into pieces and put in broth. Add tomatoes and chilies, cumin, and both soups.

2. In a skillet, sauté onions and bell peppers in 1 tablespoon oil over medium heat. Add to soup pot along with chicken. Stir and cook for about 10 minutes. Stir frequently so it won't burn.

3. Whisk together evaporated milk and cornstarch, and slowly add to soup. Cook another 2–3 minutes or until thick and bubbly.

Basil Tomato Soup

When John had to return to the United States from Africa due to a family emergency, the kids and I stayed at the SIL Conference Center. We were extremely busy and closing out our ministry, and three different families brought us dinner that week. The funny thing was that everyone brought us homemade tomato soup and some kind of homemade bread!

—Suzanne—

½ onion, finely chopped

2 tablespoons margarine

3 tablespoons flour

1 teaspoon salt

½ teaspoon pepper

1 teaspoon basil

Dash of garlic powder

2 cups tomato juice

2 cups cold milk

In a saucepan, sauté onion in margarine over medium heat. Whisk in flour, salt, pepper, basil, garlic powder, and tomato juice. Boil for 1 minute. Add milk and heat until almost boiling.

Spicy Smoked Chicken Noodle Soup

This is my all-time favorite chicken soup, because I love spicy foods and don't care much for bland canned chicken noodle soup. This has enough zip to it that I really enjoy it. If you don't have leftover smoked chicken, half of a rotisserie chicken will work.

—Suzanne—

½ skin-on smoked chicken or rotisserie chicken

½ cup finely chopped carrots

½ cup finely chopped onion

2 bouillon cubes

½ teaspoon pepper

2 ounces uncooked spaghetti, broken up

1. Put chicken in a pot and cover with water. Simmer for 30–45 minutes or until chicken is falling off the bones. Remove chicken. Discard bones and skin, and chop chicken. You will have a really tasty broth.
2. Add chicken and remaining ingredients to broth, and simmer for 30 minutes or until carrots are tender.

Open-a-Can Meatless Taco Soup

Some nights you just don't have time to defrost anything, but you want a hot dinner for your family. This soup will fit the bill. Open a few cans, mix, heat, and you have a ready meal. You can round it out with some crackers, cheesy quesadillas, or Fritos.

—Martha—

2 14½-ounce cans diced tomatoes with green pepper and onion

1 16-ounce can shoe peg corn

1 15-ounce can red beans

1 15-ounce can pinto beans

1 15-ounce can black beans

1 onion chopped (or ¼ cup dried chopped onion)

1 14½-ounce can Rotel, either spicy or mild

1 envelope dried ranch dressing mix

1 envelope taco seasoning mix

Do not drain any of the cans! Mix all the ingredients together in a large nonstick pot over medium to low heat. Cook until onion is soft. Be sure to stir occasionally so that it does not stick.

Serve with tortilla chips or crackers.

Zesty Taco Soup

I love taco soup! I am not a big soup fan, but taco soup is in a class of its own. This recipe makes a huge batch, so you can freeze half of it. Not long ago we were having a soup and salad dessert fellowship with our Sunday School class. It was a rainy, dreary night, and only three of us showed up. One had made this soup, another biscuits, and the third dessert. We couldn't have planned it any better!

—Suzanne—

2 pounds ground beef

1 large onion diced

1 bell pepper diced

2 cloves garlic, crushed

2 envelopes taco seasoning

1 envelope dry ranch dressing mix

1 16-ounce can black beans

1 28-ounce can crushed tomatoes

1 15-ounce can whole kernel corn

6 cups water

Shredded Cheddar cheese

In a saucepan over medium heat, brown ground beef, onion, pepper, and garlic. Drain. Add seasoning mixes, black beans, tomatoes, corn, and 6 cups water. Simmer on low heat for 30 minutes. Serve with Cheddar cheese to sprinkle on top.

I have not stopped thanking God for you. I pray for you constantly.

—EPHESIANS 1:16

Creamy Chicken Noodle Soup

There has been a lot written about the healing property of chicken noodle soup. In Togo we did not have sandwich meat readily available, so I often made soup and cornbread for lunches. One of my family's favorites is chicken noodle soup. Because I make it so often, I have several versions with very different consistencies and tastes. This is probably the kid's favorite because they like things bland and creamy.

—Suzanne—

½ chicken, stewed

2 quarts water

4 chicken bouillon cubes

1 16-ounce bag frozen peas and carrots

4 ounces uncooked egg noodles

2 cups milk

4 tablespoons flour

Salt and pepper to taste

1. Stew chicken over medium heat in 2 quarts of water for about 1 hour until it falls off the bones. Debone and chop chicken. Discard bones. Dissolve bouillon cubes in the chicken broth. Add frozen vegetables, chicken, and egg noodles to the broth. Cook for 30 minutes.
2. Whisk together milk and flour. Slowly add to chicken soup mixture, whisking the whole time so it doesn't get lumpy. Simmer another 5–10 minutes or until rich and creamy. Season with salt and pepper to taste.

Mammy's Vegetable Beef Soup

John loves this easy vegetable soup. His grandmother, called Mammy, always made it with lots of garden fresh vegetables. I use frozen, but it always hits the spot, especially with a fresh batch of cornbread or muffins! One of my treasures is Mammy's soup pot. I inherited it a few years ago, and soup definitely tastes better cooked in it.

—Suzanne—

1 pound stew meat

1 tablespoon vegetable oil

1 quart water

1 16-ounce bag frozen vegetables

1 large onion, diced

1 28-ounce can diced tomatoes

1 16-ounce can corn

1 8-ounce can tomato sauce

½ cup macaroni noodles, uncooked (optional)

Salt and pepper to taste

1. In a large soup pot or Dutch oven, brown stew meat in oil over medium heat.
Add 1 quart water. Simmer for 30 minutes.
2. Add frozen vegetables, onion, diced tomatoes, corn, and tomato sauce, and simmer for 1 hour.
Add noodles and cook 10 minutes. Add salt and pepper to taste.

Middle Eastern Lentil Soup

In Togo, I really struggled to find quick things to fix for lunch. I usually cooked a big homemade dinner and was busy during the day. Sandwich meat was hard to come by, and we usually made our own bread, so sandwiches were not a quick and easy option. This soup became one of our favorites since lentils don't have to be soaked, and they cook relatively quickly.

—Suzanne—

1 cup lentils

4 cups water

1½ teaspoons cumin

1 tablespoon olive oil

1 onion, chopped

3 cloves garlic, crushed

1 tablespoon flour

2 tablespoons lemon juice

Salt and pepper to taste

Dollop plain yogurt or sour cream

1. In a soup pot, add lentils, water, and cumin, bring to boil, then simmer for 45 minutes or until lentils are soft.
2. In skillet over medium heat, add olive oil, onions, and garlic; sauté until soft. Add flour to skillet, and stir to combine.
3. Add sautéed ingredients to lentils, and stir until flour is well blended. Boil for 5 minutes. Remove from heat and add lemon juice; season with salt and pepper. Serve with a dollop of either plain yogurt or sour cream.

Potato Soup

I had never tried potato soup—it didn't sound very appetizing to me. Then one winter our senior pastor's wife cooked a big pot of potato soup for all the other staff wives at the church. She had everything set up beautifully with a lovely salad, fresh bread, and toppings for our soup. I tried a bowl and absolutely loved it!

—Suzanne—

SOUP
1 onion, finely chopped

2 tablespoons oil

1 tablespoon flour

1 teaspoon salt

Dash pepper

1 cup water

1 cup leftover mashed potatoes

2½ cups milk

1 cup shredded sharp Cheddar cheese

TOPPINGS
Sliced green onions

Crumbled, cooked bacon

Sour cream

Grated cheese

1. In a medium soup pot over medium heat, sauté onion in oil. Blend in flour, salt, and pepper.
2. Add water and cook 2 minutes, stirring constantly. Add potatoes, milk, and Cheddar cheese, and heat until almost boiling.
3. Serve with toppings so everyone can garnish their bowl.

Don't worry about anything; instead, pray about everything. Tell God what you need, and thank him for all he has done. Then you will experience God's peace, which exceeds anything we can understand. His peace will guard your hearts and minds as you live in Christ Jesus.

—PHILIPPIANS 4:6–7

Antipasti Salad Arranged on Individual Plates

When I was a young bride living in student housing, I had some beautiful green Fostoria plates and glasses I had gotten as wedding presents. I thought the plates were so beautiful that I would arrange things on them for the salad course when friends came over. We only had a card table for eating, so I would get out my best tablecloth, our grape china, and the green glasses. Then I would place the salad items on my beautiful green salad plates, just like Mama and Daddy had always done when they entertained important New York guests when they were living in New Jersey. I was not old enough to remember this, but Mama told me about the antipasti platters and all of the goodies she arranged on them.

—Martha—

Italian dressing	Pieces of celery	Pickled mushrooms
Lettuce leaves	Radishes	Sliced, boiled eggs
1 6-ounce can ripe olives, drained	Tomato sections	Green olives
1 cucumber, peeled, scored, and sliced thin	Red, green, orange, or yellow peppers	Pimento pieces
Thin slices provolone cheese	Pickled beets	Hot banana peppers
Thin slices salami	Ham slivers	Pickled cauliflower
1 2-ounce can rolled anchovy fillets	Prosciutto ham	Green pepper rings
		Green olives

For making my antipasti salad, I simply used whatever choices I had available with lettuce underneath. When I could afford a can of rolled anchovies, I used a few on each plate. Somehow, I always thought anchovies were elegant. I still do. Radishes were the least expensive "red" ingredient and always added such color to the plate. Just pick and choose what you have available of the above ingredients and arrange attractively on individual plates.

Broccoli, Bacon, and Raisin Salad

Broccoli, Bacon, and Raisin Salad

I first had this salad when John and I were in seminary. We were living on our very tight $20-a-week budget, and when a friend fixed this for a potluck it seemed like such an exotic, expensive dish. Bacon and fresh broccoli in a side dish? It was heavenly!

—Suzanne—

SALAD
2 bunches broccoli crowns

2 cups golden raisins

1 cup pecans, chopped

1½ cups chopped crisp bacon

DRESSING
1½ cups mayonnaise

1 cup red wine vinegar

¾ cup sugar

Mix broccoli, raisins, and pecans, and chill overnight. Mix dressing ingredients and refrigerate for at least 1 hour. Just before serving, stir in bacon and dressing.

Red and Green Layered Salad

*This beautiful salad is as pretty as it is tasty. It looks great in a glass bowl or trifle dish.
I think it is very special to layer salads where the different ingredients are visible.
I love to look at cooking magazines, and it seems that the test kitchen cooks
and/or their food stylists know just how to make things beautiful. I found that
this salad layered in my trifle bowl always brings rave reviews. You can make
a salad as pretty as the ones in the magazines if you just let the artist in you
come through when making your layers.*

—Martha—

4 eggs

½ head shredded lettuce

1 red onion, chopped

3 stalks celery, diced

1 can water chestnuts, drained

1 bunch radishes, sliced

1 small package frozen peas

2 cups mayonnaise

Salt and pepper to taste

4 slices bacon, crumbled

Parmesan cheese, grated

1. In a medium saucepan, bring 4 cups water (or enough to cover fully cover the eggs; amount will vary
depending on the size of saucepan used) to boil, carefully add eggs, then reduce to simmer;
cook 14 minutes. Remove eggs to a bowl of cold water, chill, then remove and slice.
2. In a glass bowl, make layers of lettuce, onions, celery, chestnuts, radishes, peas,
and mayonnaise. Be sure mayonnaise is on the top layer. Garnish with egg slices,
salt and pepper, crumbled bacon, and grated Parmesan cheese.

Red and Green Layered Salad

Dijon Avocado Tomato Salad

This is another favorite from Togo that translates well to dinner here. During avocado season, the market ladies would stack up three to five large avocados. These delectable, right-off-the-tree snacks would cost about $1 per stack. I have never found avocados that taste the same here in the United States. It must be something about being picked ripe off the tree.

—Suzanne—

2 or 3 avocados, diced

3 Roma tomatoes, diced

½ bunch green onions, sliced

3 tablespoons Dijon mustard

3 tablespoons oil

½ teaspoon salt

¼ teaspoon pepper

1 tablespoon soy sauce

2 cloves fresh garlic, peeled and coarsely chopped

¼ cup water

Place avocados, tomatoes, and onions in a bowl. Place remaining ingredients in blender and whirl on high for 1 minute. Mix with vegetables and chill. Incredible! This is definitely not guacamole.

A bowl of vegetables with someone you love is better than steak with someone you hate.

—PROVERBS 15:17

Tabbouleh

This Middle Eastern couscous salad was a big favorite in Togo. My friend, Gaye, brought it to Thanksgiving dinner one year. The tartness of the lime mixed with the olive oil and couscous makes it a cold and refreshing salad on a hot day. This salad is truly beautiful as well as super delicious. You really need to try this one!

—Suzanne—

DRESSING
½ cup olive oil

4 tablespoons lime juice

2 cloves garlic, crushed

1½ teaspoons salt

¼ teaspoon pepper

SALAD
2 cups water

1 16-ounce box couscous

1 cucumber, diced

1 bunch fresh parsley, snipped

4 Roma tomatoes, diced

1 bunch green onions, sliced

1. Place all dressing ingredients in blender and whirl for 30 seconds.
2. Boil 2 cups water. Turn off heat and pour in entire box of couscous. Let sit for 5 minutes, and then fluff with fork. Let couscous cool, and then toss with vegetables. Add dressing. It is best if it sits in refrigerator overnight to let flavors marinate.

Tangy Sweet Coleslaw

Cabbage was a seasonal vegetable in Togo. When the weather was really dry and the Harmattan winds were blowing off the desert, all the vegetables began to taste bitter, except for cabbage. During the dry, dusty days of Harmattan, this coleslaw was a staple at our dinner table.

—Suzanne—

½ head crisp cabbage, finely chopped

2 carrots, shredded

½ cup mayonnaise

¼ cup milk

2 tablespoons vinegar

½ cup sugar

½ teaspoon salt

⅛ teaspoon pepper

Place the cabbage and carrots in a 1-gallon zipper bag. Whisk remaining ingredients in a bowl and pour over the cabbage mix. Let chill in refrigerator for at least 2 hours; turn bag occasionally to let the dressing marinate all of the cabbage. **Note:** You can substitute a 16-ounce bag of coleslaw mix for the cabbage and carrots to save time.

Mandarin Orange Spinach Salad

Nothing tastes as good in the summer as a cold, crisp salad. The fruit in this salad makes it especially refreshing. My family loves mandarin oranges and strawberries, and I love knowing that I have found a way to have them eating spinach—just mix them all together!

—Suzanne—

1 11-ounce can mandarin oranges, reserve juice

¼ cup extra-virgin olive oil

3 tablespoons raspberry jam or spreadable fruit

1 tablespoon red wine vinegar

2 tablespoons poppy seeds

1 bag spinach

1 cup strawberries, sliced

1 cup sliced almonds, toasted

1. Mix ½ cup of juice drained from oranges, oil, jam, red wine vinegar, and poppy seeds. Chill for at least 1 hour.

2. Just before serving, toss together mandarin oranges, spinach, strawberries, and toasted almonds. Serve with the dressing.

I know how to live on almost nothing or with everything. I have learned the secret of living in every situation, whether it is with a full stomach or empty, with plenty or little.

—PHILIPPIANS 4:12

Caesar Salad

We don't go out to eat often, but whenever I go to Italian restaurants I love to order this salad. This is a version you can make at home for your own Italian night. My children always think we have had something very special when I fix Caesar salad at home. To tell you the truth, this Caesar salad is better than most I have had in restaurants.

—Suzanne—

DRESSING
3 tablespoons extra-virgin olive oil

4½ teaspoons lemon juice

1 teaspoon prepared mustard

2 tablespoons mayonnaise

1 garlic clove, minced

SALAD
6 cups torn romaine

1 cup Caesar salad croutons

½ cup shredded Parmesan cheese

Coarsely ground pepper to taste

1. Whisk together olive oil, lemon juice, mustard, mayonnaise, and garlic. Let chill for 1 hour.
2. Mix romaine lettuce, croutons, and Parmesan cheese. Top with pepper to taste.
3. Toss with dressing and serve.

Pasadena Salad

This has been in my cooking files for many years. Truly, I don't remember why I called it Pasadena Salad. Most likely someone at one of our Martha's Extravaganzas (sewing seminars) in Pasadena gave it to me jotted on a piece of paper. It is just fabulous, and I love the name and all of the wonderful sewing memories of the Pasadena Convention Center.

—Martha—

¾ cup shrimp (1 small can)

1½ cups celery

½ cup radishes

½ cup peas

Salt and pepper to taste

½ cup mayonnaise

¼ cup nuts

1 teaspoon tarragon vinegar

1. Cut shrimp in small pieces. Dice celery. Cut radishes in thick slices.
2. Combine vegetables in a salad bowl; season with salt and pepper to taste and sprinkle vinegar over mixture. Spread mayonnaise on top, and sprinkle with chopped nuts.
3. Serve small scoops on top of lettuce leaves on plate.

Let the trees of the forest rustle with praise, for the Lord is coming to judge the earth.

—1 CHRONICLES 16:33

Strawberry Pretzel Salad

This is my very favorite congealed salad in the whole world. Blanche Miller first brought this recipe to me. Blanche worked for us when I first opened my tiny retail shop in Huntsville. She was an excellent cook and was always bringing good things to eat for the employees. After tasting this "salad" for the first time it became my favorite "salad." Now, most people would not call this a salad but rather a dessert! It is truly delicious and always brings rave reviews and I do serve it as a salad not a dessert.

—Martha—

2 cups thin pretzels, crushed

¾ cup butter, melted

1 tablespoon plus 1 cup sugar

2 10-ounce packages frozen strawberries (the sweetened kind in a box)

1 8-ounce package cream cheese

1 8-ounce carton Cool Whip

1 6-ounce package strawberry Jell-O

1½ cups boiling water

1. Preheat oven to 400°F.
2. In a medium bowl, mix pretzel crumbs, butter, and 1 tablespoon sugar. Pat into 9" x 13" baking dish. Bake 8 minutes, then cool.
3. Thaw the frozen strawberries. Beat together the cream cheese and 1 cup sugar. Stir in Cool Whip and spread on pretzel layer.
4. Combine Jell-O and boiling water. Stir in thawed strawberries and mix well. Pour over cream cheese, sugar, and Cool Whip layer.
5. Refrigerate until top layer is congealed and ready to serve.

If you help the poor, you are lending to the Lord—and he will repay you!

—PROVERBS 19:17

Strawberry Buttermilk Jell-O Salad

I know, buttermilk and Jell-O don't sound appetizing together. Trust me—I am not a buttermilk fan, but this salad completely disguises the buttermilk taste. This is one of the flavors of Thanksgiving for me, and it is another of my Aunt Peggy's recipes.

—Suzanne—

1 20-ounce can crushed pineapple

1 6-ounce package strawberry Jell-O

2 cups buttermilk

½ cup finely chopped pecans

1 12-ounce container Cool Whip

Nonstick cooking spray

1. In a saucepan over high heat, heat pineapple in its syrup to boiling point. Add Jell-O and boil for 1 minute. Pour into a medium bowl and cool.

2. Add buttermilk and chopped nuts. Carefully fold in the whipped topping.

3. Pour into a 9" x 13" glass dish coated with nonstick cooking spray. Refrigerate until set.

Fresh Fruit Salad

On Tuesday mornings we have breakfast for the ladies who come to Bible study. We alternate which class provides the food every week, and usually it is pretty heavy fare with lots of sweets, biscuits, sausage, and pastries. I have started bringing fruit salad when it's my turn. Everybody seems to really appreciate a lighter, healthier option, and it sure is good!

—Suzanne—

1 cantaloupe or honeydew, cut into chunks

1 green apple, diced

1 red apple, diced

3 fresh peaches, sliced thinly

1 fresh pineapple, cubed

1 or 2 cups seedless grapes

2 cups sliced strawberries

3 tablespoons frozen orange juice concentrate

In a large bowl, mix together fruit, then add orange juice concentrate. You can substitute other fresh fruits if desired. Stir until fruit is coated in the orange juice concentrate. Cover and refrigerate.

May we shout for joy when we hear of your victory and raise a victory banner in the name of our God. May the Lord answer all your prayers.

—PSALM 20:5

Grape Salad

This has been a hit at every luncheon and potluck I've attended. I saw it a few times before I actually tasted it, because the idea of mixing together cream cheese and grapes did not sound appealing to me. It is actually quite good! The cool, sweet cream cheese mixture really complements the grapes.

—Suzanne—

2 cups green seedless grapes

1 cup red seedless grapes

1 cup dark purple seedless grapes

1 8-ounce package cream cheese

1 12-ounce container Cool Whip

1 teaspoon vanilla

1 cup brown sugar, divided

1 cup toasted pecan pieces

1. Wash grapes and set aside. In a medium bowl, combine cream cheese, whipped topping, vanilla, and ½ cup brown sugar; mix well. Stir in grapes.

2. Put in pretty glass bowl and top with remaining ½ cup brown sugar and pecans. Cover and let sit in refrigerator overnight. The brown sugar will dissolve and form a crust on top.

Zesty Pasta Salad

This was another Togo lunch favorite. We really liked cold things for lunch! We usually didn't have the pepperoni to put in it, but we used leftover chicken or roast beef or whatever we had on hand. We mixed up our own vinaigrette, but there are many dressings readily available from your local market, which simplifies the preparation.

—Suzanne—

16 ounces ziti tricolor pasta

3 carrots, diced

1 bunch green onions, diced

5 Roma tomatoes, diced

3 bell peppers, diced

6 ounces mozzarella cheese, diced

3 ounces pepperoni, cut up

1 16-ounce bottle Kraft Zesty Italian Dressing & Marinade

Cook pasta according to package directions. Rinse, drain, and let cool. Mix with vegetables, cheese, pepperoni, and dressing.

Togolese Egg Salad Sandwiches

These sandwiches were my New Year's invention for Togo. Our family likes a little "zip" in our food, so we prefer these to traditional egg salad sandwiches.

—Suzanne—

6 hard-boiled eggs, finely diced

½ cup mayonnaise

½ cup finely chopped onion

1 or 2 tablespoons Dijon mustard

1 teaspoon salt

½ teaspoon cayenne pepper

French baguettes, sliced in half

Lettuce to taste

Mix together eggs, mayonnaise, onion, mustard, salt, and cayenne pepper. Chill for 1–2 hours, then slather egg salad on baguette halves and top with lettuce. Yummy!

The Lord is my strength and shield. I trust him with all my heart.
He helps me, and my heart is filled with joy.
I burst out in songs of thanksgiving.

—PSALM 28:7

Curried Fruit

Mama began making hot fruit dishes many years ago. When I found this curried fruit recipe, I tried it for Christmas and everyone loved it. Correction, I should say all the adults; the children weren't as smitten, but then they only eat about five different foods. The combination of fruits blended with the curry makes this a melody of tastes. This curry dish is a beautiful accompaniment not only to a Christmas dinner but also to a brunch or luncheon with lighter fare such as egg casseroles, cheese grits, or chicken salad.

—Martha—

1 16-ounce can chunk pineapple

1 jar apple rings

1 29-ounce can apricots

1 29-ounce can peaches

1 29-ounce can pears

1 20-ounce can cherries (pie cherries, not pie filling)

½ cup butter

¾ cup dark brown sugar

4 teaspoons curry powder

1. Drain all fruit. Arrange in a baking dish. (I use a large Pyrex dish.)
2. In a saucepan over medium-low heat, melt butter, then add brown sugar and curry to melted butter. Mix well, being sure all sugar lumps are gone. Spread over fruit. Cover and refrigerate overnight if possible.
3. Preheat oven to 350°F, then bake for 1 hour.

Onion Rings

In Togo there wasn't much fast food available except for a restaurant called "Al Donald's." It copied the colors and menu from McDonald's with a few very obvious differences. Al's served all their burgers with cabbage on top, and most came with a fried egg on them as well. Unless you specifically asked for French fries on the side, they came inside your hamburger bun! Fast food like this convinced us to make our own most of the time. Onion rings are a fast-food treat that are lot of work to make. Still, it is a fun, tasty project with the kids, with strict supervision around the hot oil, of course. Our favorite time to make them is when the big Vidalia onions are in season.

—Suzanne—

¾ cup plain flour

¼ cup cornstarch

½ teaspoon baking powder

¼ teaspoon baking soda

1 cup water

1 egg

Large onions cut into rings

Oil for frying

1. In a medium bowl, mix together flour, cornstarch, baking powder, baking soda, water, and egg to make batter.
2. Put a handful of onion rings in the batter at a time. Lift them out, let them drip, and put in hot oil about ½" deep in pan. Fry until golden brown, turning halfway through.

Easy Cheese Cauliflower

My boys always liked cauliflower. Joe likes cauliflower. So I fixed cauliflower reasonably often—sometimes with just butter melted on the top of the whole cauliflower. When I was given this special version of cauliflower, it was a hit with all my cauliflower lovers. A lot of things simply taste better with cheese melted on top.

—Martha—

1 head cauliflower

½ cup mayonnaise

2 teaspoons prepared mustard

Salt and pepper to taste

¾ cup shredded sharp Cheddar cheese

1. Bring a large stockpot filled about halfway with water to a boil, add whole cauliflower, reduce to a simmer, and cook for 20–25 minutes. Drain well, then place in shallow baking dish.

2. Preheat oven to 350°F. Mix together mayonnaise, mustard, salt, and pepper, and spread on top of hot cauliflower. Sprinkle cheese on top and bake until cheese melts, about 8–12 minutes.

Bacon Green Bean Bundles

My daughter-in-law, Sherry Anne, makes this wonderful side dish for many occasions. The bacon complements the green beans, and it looks very elegant.

—Martha—

1 pound fresh green beans, trimmed

8 bacon strips, partially cooked

1 tablespoon finely chopped onion

3 tablespoons butter

1 tablespoon white wine vinegar

¼ teaspoon salt

1 tablespoon sugar

1. Preheat oven to 400°F. Boil beans until tender crisp, about 5 minutes; drain.

2. Arrange the beans in little bundles and wrap in bacon. Secure with a toothpick. Bake on a foil-lined cookie sheet for 15 minutes.

3. In a saucepan, heat onion, butter, vinegar, salt, and sugar until boiling. Put bean bundles on platter and drizzle with sauce.

Spinach Casserole with Cheese

Mama always cooked vegetable casseroles for special occasions. For ordinary family meals we just had vegetables cooked with a little butter, olive oil, or salt pork. She used canned or frozen vegetables except in the summer when my grandmother and granddaddy had a huge garden. We had a table laden with fresh vegetables every day during the summer. She loved to can and freeze those fresh vegetables to use all winter. This casserole is good to make a day ahead, refrigerate, and cook the next day. For my big Christmas and Thanksgiving dinners, I really like to prepare ahead and just pop everything into the oven on the big day. You might need to adjust your baking time slightly if you're starting from a cold state.

—Martha—

2 10-ounce packages frozen chopped spinach

8 ounces sour cream

2 tablespoons dry onion soup mix

1 cup shredded sharp Cheddar cheese

1. Preheat oven to 350°F. Cook spinach according to package directions, and drain well.
2. Combine spinach, sour cream, and onion soup mix. Spoon into a lightly greased, 1-quart casserole dish. Sprinkle cheese on top. Bake for 25 minutes.

Togolese Spinach

When we first went to Togo, I despised spinach. I knew Popeye loved it and it was healthy for me, but I didn't think I would ever learn to like it. Then a friend fixed this rich garlicky spinach, and it changed my opinion of this leafy vegetable.

—Suzanne—

2 tablespoons olive oil

1 onion, diced

3 cloves garlic, crushed

4 Roma tomatoes, diced

¼ teaspoon salt

1 bunch spinach

Prepared rice (optional)

1. Warm oil in skillet over medium heat. Add onion and garlic and cook until translucent.
2. Add tomato and salt to mix. Simmer for one minute. Add spinach and cook until wilted. Serve with rice or by itself.

Fear of the Lord leads to life, bringing security and protection from harm.

—PROVERBS 19:23

Ritz Cracker
Broccoli Casserole

Ritz cracker casseroles held a prominent place in Mama's special occasion cooking. She cooked special meals not only at Christmas and Thanksgiving but also for Mother's and Father's Days, Easter, and birthdays. Since Daddy travelled during the week, Mama made wonderful things all weekend knowing full well that he had to eat in restaurants most of the time. The recipe ingredients I have given you below are for a family-size version, not a Christmas dinner size. If you want a larger casserole, please double the given ingredients.

—Martha—

1 10-ounce box frozen chopped broccoli

½ cup cream of mushroom or celery soup

1 egg, beaten

½ cup grated sharp Cheddar cheese

½ cup mayonnaise

1 small onion, chopped

Salt and pepper to taste

30 Ritz Crackers

½ stick butter

1. Preheat oven to 350°F. Cook broccoli according to package directions, then drain. Mix with remaining ingredients, except crackers and butter, and pour into baking dish.
2. Top with crushed Ritz Crackers and dot with butter. Bake uncovered for about 45 minutes.

Spicy Cubed Potatoes

Mom Pullen used to make these potatoes when we would come to visit. They are so easy and are something different from plain, bland potatoes.

—Suzanne—

6 potatoes, cubed

1 onion, diced

2 tablespoons Cajun seasoning

3 tablespoons oil

Preheat oven to 425°F. Arrange potatoes and onions in a greased casserole dish. Sprinkle liberally with Cajun seasoning. Pour oil over the top and stir. Bake for 45 minutes or until potatoes are tender.

Yummy Mashed Potatoes

I love mashed potatoes. We had them occasionally when I was growing up. At family gatherings my grandchildren always request mashed potatoes, period. This recipe is one I have had for many years, and it makes mashed potatoes a little bit fancier than the ordinary potatoes, milk, and butter.

—Martha—

6 medium potatoes, quartered

3 ounces cream cheese

8 ounces sour cream with chives

½ stick butter

Paprika

1. In a medium stockpot, cover potatoes with water, bring to a boil, and cook for 15–20 minutes or until fork tender; drain and mash. While potatoes are cooking, preheat oven to 350°F.

2. Stir cream cheese and sour cream into potatoes. Put in lightly greased, oblong casserole dish and dot with butter. Sprinkle lightly with paprika and bake for 20 minutes.

Sausage Baked Beans

Every time I'm invited to a summer barbecue my friends ask me to bring these beans. With all the meat in them, they can almost serve as a meal alone.

—Suzanne—

1 pound breakfast sausage (I usually use hot and spicy.)

2 onions, diced

3 16-ounce cans pork and beans

½ cup ketchup

½ cup brown sugar

3 tablespoons mustard

2 tablespoons lemon juice or vinegar

¼ cup maple syrup

Preheat oven to 375°F. In a skillet over medium heat, add the sausage and onion and cook until sausage browns. Put this cooked mixture and all the remaining ingredients in a 9" x 13" pan and mix well. Bake for 1 hour.

Mozzarella Broiled Tomatoes

On our anniversary John and I love to go to Cowan, Tennessee. We always eat at an incredible Italian restaurant around the corner from our bed and breakfast. One of their most popular side dishes is a hot tomato dish. John and I enjoyed it so much that I came home and experimented until it tasted just "right."

—Suzanne—

1 pound ripe tomatoes

1 teaspoon Italian seasoning

½ teaspoon garlic salt

¼ teaspoon pepper

2 cups grated mozzarella cheese

Place the tomatoes in a greased casserole dish and sprinkle with spices. Top with cheese and broil for about 5 minutes until hot and bubbly.

Parmesan Potatoes

*This is one of my favorite ways to cook potatoes. They complement almost any meal.
When I first started cooking I thought they were the ultimate in elegance.
Now I cook potatoes in more elegant ways, but I still love the unique
taste of these Parmesan potatoes.*

—Suzanne—

5 potatoes

½ cup Parmesan cheese

1 teaspoon salt

½ teaspoon pepper

½ teaspoon paprika

1 teaspoon basil

1 teaspoon parsley

¼ cup flour

1 stick butter

1. Preheat oven to 400°F. Slice potatoes in thick slices with peel on. In a resealable bag, mix cheese, spices, and flour. Put potatoes in the bag and shake to coat.
2. Pour potatoes in a greased 9" x 13" baking dish. Melt butter and pour it over the potatoes. Bake for 1 hour or until potatoes are tender.

Restore to me the joy of your salvation, and make me willing to obey you.

—PSALM 51:12

Sweet Potato Marshmallow Casserole

Sweet Potato Marshmallow Casserole

What holiday is complete without a good dose of sweet potatoes and marshmallows? This sweet and gooey "vegetable" dish is Southern to its core.

—Martha—

4 large sweet potatoes

1½ cups milk

½ stick butter

½ cup brown sugar

2 teaspoons cinnamon

2 eggs

1 16-ounce bag marshmallows

1. Peel and slice sweet potatoes. Add to stockpot, add water to cover, and boil for 25–30 minutes or until tender. Preheat oven to 350°F.
2. Put potatoes in mixing bowl with all remaining ingredients except marshmallows. Beat until potatoes are well mashed and remaining ingredients well blended.
3. Pour into a greased 9" x 13" dish and bake for 30 minutes. Top with marshmallows and bake another 15 minutes.

Cold Vegetable Medley

The sweet and tangy marinade combined with the crunch of these vegetables makes this a very special side dish for any meal. It's especially good and refreshing during the hot summer days. I have always loved dishes that could be made ahead and put in the refrigerator. This is one of those healthy refrigerator dishes. It is also very pretty with the colors of orange, white, brown, and green. I might add that Mama was very big on "do ahead" dishes since she taught school and loved to have part of the dinner already waiting when she got home.

—Martha—

1 green bell pepper

1 head cauliflower, separated into florets

1 head broccoli, separated into florets

8 ounces fresh mushrooms

1 8-ounce bag baby carrots

1 celery bunch, sliced into ½" slices

2 cloves garlic, crushed

1½ cups red wine vinegar

½ cup sugar

2 tablespoons prepared mustard

2 teaspoons salt

1 teaspoon oregano leaves

Pepper to taste

In a medium bowl, mix together all vegetables. In a small bowl, mix remaining ingredients into a sauce and pour over the veggies. Refrigerate overnight before serving.

Zesty Grilled Potatoes

*I love anything cooked on the grill, even potatoes. The dressing gives them
a lot of zip, and cooking them on the grill gives them the perfect finish.
This is also a great way to use leftover baked potatoes.*

—Martha—

4 large Idaho potatoes

1 8-ounce bottle of Kraft Zesty Italian Dressing & Marinade

Salt and pepper

1. Scrub potatoes, place in a large stockpot, and cover with cold water. Boil until slightly tender,
approximately 20 minutes (toothpick will insert easily).
Remove potatoes from water and let cool.

2. Slice approximately ⅜" thick. Place in a shallow dish and cover with dressing.
Marinate at least 1 hour.

3. Place on grill and sprinkle with salt and pepper. Grill on each side until slightly browned.

*Many waters cannot quench love, nor can rivers drown it.
If a man tried to buy love with all his wealth,
his offer would be utterly scorned.*

—SONG OF SOLOMON 8:7

Cabbage Potato Salad

I have served this potato salad for many years. It has a wonderful crunch. Since I really like cabbage and bell peppers, the combination adds just the right touch to traditional potato salad. I always use low-fat or fat-free mayonnaise. You will have to decide if you like this with the no-fat version. If you use fat-free mayonnaise, the calories will be reduced tremendously. If you really wanted to "healthy it up," slice your boiled eggs and remove most of the yolk, only layering the whites of the eggs. I love this because it is not a traditionally squishy potato salad. Joe loves this version and has never liked "stirred up" potato salad. It is especially pretty made in a clear glass trifle bowl.

—Martha—

8–10 medium white potatoes	Celery seed to taste	12 hard-boiled eggs, sliced
1 head cabbage, shredded	4 red onions, sliced and in rings	1 1-quart jar mayonnaise
Salt and pepper for each layer	1 each green, red, orange, and yellow peppers, cut in rings	Paprika for top

1. In a large stockpot, add potatoes (with skins on) and enough cold water to cover. Bring to boil, then reduce heat to simmer and cook for approximately 20 minutes until slightly tender (toothpick will insert easily). Slice them in ⅛"–¼" rounds.

2. Begin layering ingredients in glass bowl as follows: a layer of shredded cabbage followed by a layer of sliced potatoes; sprinkle with salt, pepper, and celery seed; add onion rings and pepper rings; add sliced hard-boiled eggs; spread mayonnaise all over, being sure to cover layers. Continue with additional layers ending with the eggs and mayonnaise. Top with paprika. Refrigerate 24 hours for best blending of flavors.

Holiday Marinated Cold Vegetables

Nearly every Mother's Day my mother would fix this dish since it could be made the day before. We always went to church on Sunday morning, and we would get a corsage (red if one's mother was alive, and white if one's mother had passed). The men in our family would wear a boutonniere also in either red or white to honor their mothers. My grandparents would come to our house for Mother's Day dinner, and we would have presents for both my Mama and my Nannie. Mother's Day was a big celebration at our house, as was Father's Day.

—Martha—

1 16-ounce can French-style green beans

1 16-ounce can English peas

1 16-ounce can white shoe peg corn

1 2-ounce jar pimento, chopped

1 cup chopped green pepper

1 cup chopped celery

1 cup chopped green onion

1 teaspoon salt

1 teaspoon pepper

1 tablespoon water

1 tablespoon vinegar

½ cup vegetable oil

4 teaspoons Splenda

1. Drain all the canned vegetables and combine in a bowl with the green pepper, celery, and onion.
2. In a saucepan, add the salt, pepper, water, vinegar, oil, and Splenda, and bring to a full boil. Let cool, and then add to the vegetables. Marinate overnight.

Mama's Sweet Potato Surprise Balls

We loved sweet potatoes, and Mama fixed them almost every way possible, from baking to her famous Sweet Potato Marshmallow Casserole for Thanksgiving and Christmas meals. We also had sweet potatoes for Easter. The surprise is the marshmallow in the center.

—Martha—

1 egg

2 cups mashed sweet potatoes

2 tablespoons sugar

½ teaspoon salt

1 16-ounce bag marshmallows

½ cup crushed corn flakes

Preheat oven to 375°F. Beat egg slightly. In a medium bowl, combine potatoes, egg, sugar, and salt. Shape into balls with a marshmallow stuffed inside each ball. Roll in cornflakes. Place on greased baking sheet and bake for 20 minutes.

Mary's Hash Brown Casserole

I was at my sister Mary's house for a special occasion when she first served this dish. I have fixed it many times, and it is always a total crowd pleaser. Men, women, and children love it.

—Martha—

½ can evaporated milk

1 large bag frozen hash brown potatoes

1 10½-ounce can cream of chicken soup

16 ounces sour cream

1 medium onion, chopped

1 stick margarine, melted

2 cups shredded Cheddar cheese

Salt and pepper to taste

1 tablespoon parsley

½ cup crushed cornflakes

1. Preheat oven to 400°F. In a medium bowl, mix all ingredients except cornflakes. Pour into 9" x 13" pan, and top with crushed cornflakes.

2. Bake for 40 minutes covered, reduce to 350°F, and bake for 40 minutes uncovered. This is a great dish for those cold winter nights.

Mary's Tomato Grits

My sister, Mary, is an incredible cook. This is one of her brunch dishes. For those of you who don't live in the South, you may have to look in the ethnic foods section in your grocery store for grits, but they are worth the time spent searching. Grits are totally Southern, and they are so good!

—Martha—

2 cups water	½ cup plus 1 tablespoon butter	2½ cups shredded Cheddar cheese
1¼ cups milk	¼ cup diced green onions	1 10-ounce can diced tomatoes and green chilies
1 teaspoon salt	4 ounces Velveeta	
1 cup quick-cooking grits	¼ teaspoon garlic powder	

1. Preheat oven to 350°F.
2. In a saucepan, bring water and milk to a boil. Add salt, then slowly add grits and return to a boil, stirring constantly for 1 minute. Reduce the heat, cover, and cook for 3 minutes.
3. Add the ½ cup butter and stir until butter is melted. Cover and cook for 3–5 minutes, or until the grits are thick and creamy. Remove from heat and set aside.
4. In a skillet over medium heat, sauté the onions in the remaining 1 tablespoon butter for 1 minute; add to grits. Add the Velveeta, garlic powder, and 1½ cups Cheddar cheese to grits, and stir until the cheese is melted. Add the tomatoes and mix well.
5. Pour the grits into a greased 8" x 11" casserole, and bake for 40 minutes. Sprinkle remaining 1 cup cheese over the casserole for the last 5 minutes of cooking time.

You made all the delicate, inner parts of my body and knit me together in my mother's womb. Thank you for making me so wonderfully complex! Your workmanship is marvelous—how well I know it.

—PSALM 139:13–14

Mama's Macaroni and Cheese

*We always loved macaroni and cheese, though Mama did not make it too often.
I think it was a bit fattening. Most of my grandchildren adore macaroni and cheese,
and most think of the Kraft box when I mention it. For all of our Thanksgiving
and Christmas dinners, the two most requested foods from my "grands" are mashed
potatoes and macaroni and cheese. The men mostly request turnip greens.
Go figure. Well, we are in the South!*

—Martha—

1 8-ounce package elbow macaroni

2 cups milk

1 egg

¾ teaspoon salt

1 cup grated sharp Cheddar cheese

¼ cup dry bread crumbs

4 tablespoons butter

1. Preheat oven to 350°F.
2. Cook macaroni according to package instructions until it's slightly undercooked,
drain, then pour into a greased casserole dish.
3. In a small mixing bowl, beat together milk, egg, and salt, then pour over macaroni.
Mix ¾ cup cheese into this mixture.
4. In a small bowl, work ¼ cup cheese and 2 tablespoons butter into bread crumbs.
Sprinkle on top of macaroni and top with pads of butter.
Bake for about 20 minutes.

Mama's Macaroni and Cheese

Butternut Squash Casserole

This is one of those tastes that always reminds me of the holidays. I don't remember ever having Thanksgiving and Christmas without this dish. When we lived in Togo, we couldn't always get butternut squash—in fact, I only remember getting it once. Instead, I used pumpkin-like vegetables that I found in the market and added a little food coloring to make them orange. It worked, and Thanksgiving still tasted like Thanksgiving.

—Suzanne—

SQUASH	TOPPING
3 cups butternut squash, diced	½ cup brown sugar
1 cup sugar	¼ cup flour
2 eggs	¼ cup butter, softened
2 teaspoons vanilla	½ cup chopped pecans
¼ cup melted butter	

1. Preheat oven to 350°F.
2. In a medium stockpot, add squash and enough water to cover, bring to a boil, and cook for 2–4 minutes or until tender crisp. Drain and mash squash.
3. In a medium bowl, mix together the squash, sugar, eggs, vanilla, and melted butter. Pour into a greased 2-quart casserole dish. Mix together topping ingredients and sprinkle on top. Bake until bubbly, about 30–40 minutes.

O Lord, you have examined my heart and know everything about me.

—PSALM 139:1

THE SCHOOL HOUSE SOUP

—Martha—

Then Jesus called for the children and said to the disciples, "Let the children come to me. Don't stop them! For the Kingdom of God belongs to those who are like these children."

—LUKE 18:16

My grandmother, Martha Isabelle Baker Dicus, and my grandfather, Leonard Houston Dicus, were two of the main influences in my life. One of my favorite cooking stories took place in the 1930s during the worst of the Great Depression in the one-room schoolhouse where my grandmother was the teacher. My grandmother was brilliant and accomplished. Born in the 1890s, she began teaching in Alabama in 1908 when she was sixteen years old. After passing the Alabama Teacher's Test, she began teaching in a schoolhouse with six grades and (if my memory serves me correctly) more than fifty children in one room. I can certainly imagine that Miss Baker had to be pretty strict! She married Leonard Houston Dicus and kept right on teaching even after having two children, my Mama, Anna Ruth, and my Uncle George. In that era, teaching after becoming a mother was a daring thing in itself. Most married women with children simply did not work outside the home. But Nannie was no ordinary woman. She even cut her hair as soon as

women began to realize that short hair was easier and more contemporary—scandalous!

During the Depression, Alabama rural areas felt the pain as much if not more than any other part of the country. My grandmother taught school for three years during that time for no money. When I was finishing my PhD in education, long after my grandmother retired, I was working on a paper and asked her, "Why did you work for three whole years for no money?" She was indignant and shook her finger at me saying these words, "Young lady, what do you mean why did I teach for no money for three years? The State of Alabama had no money, and the children had to have an education." I quickly learned never to ask my grandmother questions like that again. That statement reminded me of who I am and of the rock-solid Christian people from whom I am descended.

Nannie realized that many of the children in their school had no food at home. She called a meeting of the parents in the area who were excellent farmers and who had canned food put away for the winter and said, "We have to have breakfast, lunch, and late afternoon food for these children because there is nothing or nearly nothing at their homes. They are coming to school hungry." My grandmother got a large pot and told the families to send any leftover food that they had from breakfast like biscuits or bits of meat. The families sent in canned goods, such as tomatoes, and beans, to be stored in the back of the classroom. Nannie always went to school early to build the fire so the classroom would be warm. She also made a pot of soup for the children every day during those hard years.

About 9 o'clock each day she would say, "That soup smells so good. Would anyone like a little bowl?" The children from the families that didn't have breakfast always got up, and Nannie served them some soup as well as the leftover breakfast items. At lunch, every child ate the soup. Right as school was ending for the day Nannie would say, "Now children, there is a horrible depression going on. We must not waste food, and there is still some soup left. Who will eat this soup so it won't go to waste?" The children who knew there would be not much supper, if any, at home ate more soup before walking home that afternoon.

When we are willing to care for children, we are acting like Jesus. He always had time for children, no matter what else was going on around him. It is important that we care for the little ones who are brought into our path and try to help them in spite of our business.

Tell Your Story

1. Have you ever been hungry or been around other people who really didn't have food? Write about that. How has this experience affected you? _____

_____

2. What have you done to care for children or others less fortunate than you? How are others different because of your care for them? _____

_____

CABBAGE SOUP AND PRAYER

—Suzanne—

Never stop praying.

—1 THESSALONIANS 5:17

Did you know that you can change your world by prayer? Our Women on Mission group did a prayer study on the country of Moldova. It is one of the poorest countries in Europe. Very few missionaries have been able to work in that country. Our church set aside a day to study about Moldova and to pray for the country and its people. One of the things that we did was to cook food from that country for lunch. We had a wonderful day of prayer and left the meeting committed to pray for Moldova. I even went home and asked John about the possibility of sending a mission team there. I was very concerned.

Shortly afterwards, we went on a trip to Gulf Shores. That is about as far as you can get from Moldova both in culture and distance. First Baptist Orange Beach had asked us to lead their Wednesday evening service with our drama and puppets. We obliged, but no lost people come to Wednesday church, do they? Surprisingly enough, a young girl with a heavy accent was there. She was touched by the presentation and decided to become a Christian. Afterward I found out that she was an international college student here from the country of Moldova! God does answer prayer in ways we can't even imagine. I was busy trying to figure out a way to go to Moldova, and God was bringing Moldova to us! To put this idea into practice, take a look at the news today. Take time to pray for the people in a country other than our own. You have no idea what a difference your prayers may make for that country.

Tell Your Story

1. What are some of your favorite international foods? When did you put them in your repertoire of recipes? _____

2. Write out a brief prayer for one of the countries from which you have recipes. _____

CHAPTER 3

Beef & Pork

And let the peace that comes from Christ rule in your hearts. For as members of one body you are called to live in peace. And always be thankful.

—COLOSSIANS 3:15

Tarragon Beef Stroganoff

When Mom Pullen e-mailed me this recipe, I did not even own any tarragon. I went to my local grocery store, bought some, and came home to try preparing this stroganoff. It was the best I have ever tasted. The tarragon really does enhance the flavor of the meat. My whole family loved it!

—Suzanne—

1 pound top sirloin

6 tablespoons butter

½ cup chopped onions

1 4-ounce can mushrooms

½ teaspoon nutmeg

½ teaspoon tarragon

1 cup sour cream

Salt and pepper to taste

Prepared noodles

1. Cut steak into strips about ½" wide and 2" long. In a skillet over medium heat, add the beef and 3 tablespoons butter; cook until meat is browned on all sides. Remove the beef and set aside.
2. Heat pan to medium heat. Add onions to pan and brown until translucent, approximately 9–11 minutes. Remove onions to the same bowl as the meat and set aside.
3. In the same pan, melt 3 tablespoons butter, and add mushrooms. Cook about 3 minutes over medium heat.
4. Sprinkle nutmeg and tarragon on the mushrooms, then reduce heat to very low, and add the sour cream. If it is too thick, add a tablespoon of water. Do not let it simmer or boil or the sour cream will curdle. Stir in the beef and onions. Add salt and pepper to taste. Serve over noodles.

Quick Hamburger Stroganoff

I often make this quick version for my family. It is a tasty and easy dinner that all of my kids love. With a creamy sauce and noodles, it is something most young children will love!

—Suzanne—

1 tablespoon olive oil

1 onion, diced

1 bell pepper, diced

1 8-ounce package sliced mushrooms

1½ pounds lean ground beef

1 tablespoon Italian seasoning

1 10½-ounce can cream of chicken soup

16 ounces sour cream

Prepared noodles

1. Add olive oil to skillet over medium-low heat and gently cook onion, bell pepper, and mushrooms until tender. Set aside.

2. Add ground beef to skillet and cook over medium-high heat until completely brown. Add sautéed vegetables, Italian seasoning, soup, and sour cream. Heat through. Serve over noodles.

Beef Stew

What is better on a cold winter night than to serve a hearty bowl of stew? This is my sister's recipe. Mary really knows how to fix good comfort food. In my life, my baby sister, Mary, is one of my main comfort people. As a child I prayed for a "red-headed baby sister." God answered my prayer, and Mary was born when I was nine years old.

—Martha—

1 pound stew meat

Salt and pepper to taste

¼ cup flour

1 tablespoon oil

4 medium potatoes, diced

2¾ cups carrots, chopped

1 medium onion, diced

1 7-ounce can tomato sauce

1. Season meat and coat with flour. Heat oil in skillet and add prepared stew meat; brown on all sides.

2. Transfer meat to a large stew pot and cover with 4 cups boiling water. Simmer about 3 hours.

3. Add potatoes, carrots, and onions. Simmer until all vegetables are tender, then add tomato sauce and salt and pepper to taste. Simmer until ready to serve.

Joe's Stuffed Hamburgers

Joe started making these stuffed hamburgers years ago. I will give you what we stuff ours with, but the sky is the limit. Grill on an outside grill and eat with a baked potato and salad or tuck inside a great hamburger bun with sliced tomatoes, lettuce, and onion. This serves four since each hamburger has two patties. This has long been one of our family's favorite things to cook on a grill. It is almost a party in itself for everyone to choose what he/she would like in his/her hamburger and fill it to the brim. Be sure you pinch the sides together really well or it will leak. When I say "pinch," I mean really pinch and work the hamburgers together.

—Martha—

Steak sauce	Shredded Cheddar cheese	Chopped olives
8 large ground sirloin patties	Chopped green peppers	Pickle relish
Chopped onions	Jalapeño slices (if desired)	

1. Put a little steak sauce on each patty. Layer chosen ingredients in the center of one patty, place another sirloin patty on top, and pinch the edges over and over until they are sealed. If you do not pinch the edges enough, the burger will fall apart on the grill.
2. Grill on medium heat basting with steak sauce of your choice. These are very thick and usually take a long time to cook.

Study this Book of Instruction continually. Meditate on it day and night so you will be sure to obey everything written in it. Only then will you prosper and succeed in all you do.

—JOSHUA 1:8

Chinese Pepper Steak

Bell peppers were a seasonal item in Togo. We couldn't get them all year round, so when they were in season, I always tried to cook lots of recipes that called for them. This pepper steak recipe is relatively easy, and very tasty. With bell peppers available all year round, you don't have an excuse not to make it!

—Suzanne—

1½ pounds steak, cut into strips

1 tablespoon oil

1 large onion, chopped

2 cloves garlic, minced

1 cup beef broth

3 tablespoons soy sauce

2 green bell peppers, sliced

2 tablespoons cornstarch

¼ cup cold water

2 tomatoes, quartered

3 cups prepared brown rice

1. In a saucepan over medium heat, add meat and oil and cook until meat is completely browned. Add onions and cook until tender.
2. Stir in garlic, broth, and soy sauce. Cover and simmer for 15 minutes. Add green peppers and simmer 5 minutes.
3. Mix cornstarch with water. Gradually pour into meat mixture, stirring and cooking until thick. Cook for 1 minute. Add tomato and heat through. Serve over rice.

Company Beef Casserole

This was one of my mom's standard recipes when I was growing up. I think she called it this because she often fixed it when company came to the house. And as a preacher's wife, she had plenty of company!

—Suzanne—

1 pound ground beef

1 medium onion, diced

2 tablespoons butter

1½ cups uncooked elbow macaroni

1 16-ounce can diced tomatoes

1 tablespoon ketchup

1 10½-ounce can cream of mushroom soup

Salt and pepper

1 cup grated cheddar cheese

1. Preheat oven to 350°F. In a saucepan over medium-high heat, add ground beef, onion, and butter, and cook until meat is completely browned.
2. Cook macaroni in boiling water for 8 minutes and drain.
3. Mix together cooked beef and onion, macaroni, tomatoes, ketchup, and cream of mushroom soup. Salt and pepper liberally. Pour into greased casserole dish and top with cheese.

Bake for 30 minutes.

Porcupine Meatballs

Our very first house was on Lenox Road in Atlanta. We had the sweetest neighbor, Nan Whitney. She was a neighbor-grandmother to our little boys, Camp and John. She gave me the recipe for these porcupines, and I fixed them at least once a week. This recipe allowed me to fix an inexpensive and delicious meal that the boys loved.

—Martha—

½ cup uncooked white rice

1 pound ground beef

2 teaspoons minced onion

2 tablespoons chili sauce (optional)

1½ teaspoons salt

Bay leaf

2 cups tomatoes and juice (can use just juice)

Parsley (optional)

Sugar

1. Preheat oven to 350°F.
2. In a medium bowl, mix together uncooked rice, meat, onion, chili sauce, and salt. Shape into medium balls.
3. In a small bowl, add bay leaf and tomatoes, and mix to combine. Place meatballs in casserole dish and cover with tomatoes. Bake 60–80 minutes; if necessary, add a little water or juice to keep meat moist while it bakes. Top with a sprinkling of parsley and a little sugar.

Is there any encouragement from belonging to Christ? Any comfort from his love? Any fellowship together in the Spirit? Are your hearts tender and compassionate? Then make me truly happy by agreeing wholeheartedly with each other, loving one another, and working together with one mind and purpose. Don't be selfish; don't try to impress others. Be humble, thinking of others as better than yourselves. Don't look out only for your own interests, but take an interest in others, too.—**PHILIPPIANS 2:1–4**

Tater Tot Casserole

When my boys were growing up they went for any dish that included beef, potatoes, and cheese as the main ingredients. This casserole was a standby because it was so easy and inexpensive to make.

—Martha—

1½ pounds ground chuck

1 onion, minced

1 10½-ounce can cream of chicken soup

1 18-ounce package frozen tater tots

1 (10½-ounce can cream of celery soup

1 cup water

1 cup grated sharp Cheddar cheese

1. Preheat oven to 350°F. Layer uncooked hamburger meat in bottom of 9" x 13" baking pan. Sprinkle onion on top of meat. Add chicken soup, tater tots, celery soup, and water.
2. Bake 1½ hours. During the last 30 minutes of baking, top with a sprinkling of grated Cheddar cheese.

My Mom's Chili

In this recipe you'll find my mom's chili, which is very mild. Even my little Ben, who has a very tender mouth, doesn't object to it whatsoever. It is comfortable and enjoyable on a cold winter's night. Mine has a bit more spice.

—Suzanne—

1 pound ground beef

1 onion, chopped

½ bell pepper, finely chopped

2 15-ounce cans kidney beans

1 10½-ounce can tomato soup

1 8-ounce can tomato sauce

½ teaspoon chili powder

1 teaspoon salt

In a large stockpot or Dutch oven over medium-high heat, add beef, onion, and bell pepper, and cook until meat is completely browned. Add remaining ingredients plus two soup cans of water. Simmer for 1 hour. Serve warm.

Tender Country-Style Ribs

Tender Country-Style Ribs

I love having barbecues in the summertime. I usually make mashed potatoes, garlic cheese biscuits, salad, ribs, and a bunch of desserts. (My garlic cheese biscuits are very simple. I bake Pillsbury frozen biscuits for 8 minutes, melt a stick of butter with 2 tablespoons minced garlic in the microwave, put this on top of the biscuits, and then cover with Cheddar cheese. I return them to the oven for 8–10 more minutes.) Sometimes I have everybody else bring a side to make things easier. John loves to man the grill. I had always struggled with my ribs being tough until a friend showed me this easy technique to make the world's best ribs. Now they are always tender and delicious!

—Suzanne—

3 pounds country-style ribs (I prefer beef)

½ bottle Dale's Steak Seasoning

Barbecue sauce

1. Put the ribs in a pot of water that almost covers them. Add the Dale's Steak Seasoning. Simmer for 1–1½ hours or until the meat is fork tender. Then place ribs on hot grill for about 5 minutes while basting with barbecue sauce. Delicious!!

2. **Note:** If you can't get Dale's in your part of the country, order it online at *www.dalesseasoning.com*. It really has a unique flavor!

Ask me and I will and tell you remarkable secrets you do not know about things to come.

—JEREMIAH 33:3

Suzanne's Chili

My brother-in-law, Mark, actually introduced me to taco seasoning in chili.
I brought that idea home and have played with it until concocting my favorite chili.
My son, Ben, isn't as crazy about it as the rest of my crew, but we tend to like
food with a little kick!

—Suzanne—

1 pound ground beef

1 pound lean pork sausage

1 onion, diced

1 bell pepper, diced

1 4-ounce can diced green chilies

1 envelope taco seasoning

1 tablespoon chili powder

¼ teaspoon ground red pepper

3 cloves garlic

1 large can crushed tomatoes

1 8-ounce can tomato sauce

1 can black beans or kidney beans (optional)

In a large saucepan over medium-high heat, add beef, pork, onion, and bell pepper, and cook until meat is browned. Add remaining ingredients and 2 cups water, bring to boil, then reduce to simmer and cook for 1 hour, adding water as needed. It tastes even better the next day.

This is my command—be strong and courageous! Do not be afraid or discouraged. For the Lord your God is with you wherever you go.

—JOSHUA 1:9

Suzanne's Chili

Mexican Lasagna

Tired of tacos? This layered meal makes a delicious alternative. It is surprisingly quick and easy to assemble and freezes incredibly well. This is one of my favorites to carry to families in need of food after an illness. Its spiciness is sure to whet any appetite.

—Suzanne—

1 pound lean ground beef

2 envelopes taco seasoning

1 cup water

16 ounces sour cream

2 teaspoons chili powder

1 tablespoon cornmeal

12 flour tortillas

1 16-ounce jar salsa

1 bunch green onions

4 cups sharp Cheddar cheese

Add sliced black olives and black beans to meat layer (optional)

1. Preheat oven to 375°F. In a skillet over medium-high heat, add ground beef and cook until it is no longer pink.
2. Add taco seasoning and water. Simmer for 10 minutes longer.
3. Mix sour cream and chili powder in small bowl. Spray 9" x 13" pan with nonstick spray and sprinkle cornmeal in bottom.
4. Put 4 tortillas in the bottom of the pan and spread with a third of the salsa. Top this with a third of the sour cream mix, a third of the onions, and a third of the cheese. Repeat in layers two more times.
5. Bake for 40–50 minutes. Let stand for 10 minutes before cutting into squares.

Kielbasa and Bow Tie Pasta Skillet

This is a tasty and different way to cook kielbasa sausage. We usually just cook this type of sausage on the grill, but this creamy noodle recipe is a good alternative. When we lived in Africa we truly enjoyed cooking on the grill. One of the first purchases we made for a special occasion upon returning to the United States was a grill; John has become, over the years of our marriage, quite the grill king.

—Suzanne—

8 ounces bow tie pasta

1 pound fully cooked kielbasa

1 4-ounce can mushrooms, drained

3 teaspoons minced garlic

2 tablespoons butter

1 tablespoon cornstarch

1½ cups milk

1½ cups fresh snow peas

1 cup shredded Cheddar cheese

1. Cook pasta according to package directions, drain, and reserve.
2. Cut kielbasa into ¼" slices. In a medium saucepan over medium heat, sauté kielbasa, mushrooms, and garlic in butter until mushrooms start to brown, 4–6 minutes.
3. Mix cornstarch and milk until smooth. Gradually add to skillet and cook until thick.
4. Mix in pasta and snow peas. Add cheese. Cook for 3 or 4 minutes longer or until cheese is completely melted.

Quick and Easy Creamy Lasagna

As much as I love to cook, I don't always have time to do everything from scratch like I did in Togo. This recipe takes advantage of quite a few shortcuts available to us here in the United States to make a homemade dinner in minutes. It also freezes well, so I usually make this recipe in multiples.

—Suzanne—

1½ pounds ground beef

½ cup frozen diced onions

½ cup frozen diced bell pepper

2 26-ounce cans zesty-type spaghetti sauce

1 28-ounce can crushed tomatoes

1 12-ounce box oven-ready lasagna noodles

1 16-ounce sour cream (usually use fat-free)

8 ounces shredded mozzarella cheese

1. Preheat oven to 375°F. In a saucepan over medium-high heat, add beef, onions, and pepper, and cook until meat is completely browned. Drain and add spaghetti sauce, 1 spaghetti-sauce can filled with water, and tomatoes. Simmer about 5 minutes.

2. Scoop a small amount of sauce in a greased 9" x 13" pan. Top with a layer of uncooked lasagna noodles. Spread about a third of the sour cream over this. Add a third of the meat mixture to this. Repeat layers twice more.

3. Top with mozzarella cheese and cover tightly with foil. Bake for 1 hour. If you want to cook it from a frozen state, cook at 350°F for 2 hours.

Easy Pork Enchiladas

This is one of my favorites to make when I'm doing a month's worth of cooking at a time. It is pretty easy to make several batches at once, and it freezes well as long as you don't top it with sauce before freezing.

—Suzanne—

3 or 4 pounds pork shoulder

1 bag frozen sliced peppers and onions

3 tablespoons diced garlic

2 large onions, sliced

2 envelopes fajita mix

12 flour tortillas

1 large can enchilada sauce

1 7-ounce package grated Cheddar cheese

1. Put pork in slow cooker. Add frozen peppers and onions, garlic, and onions; sprinkle with dry fajita mix. Cook on medium for 8–10 hours, until meat is falling off the bones.
2. Preheat oven to 350°F. Shred meat and put it in a separate bowl along with the cooked vegetables. Place meat mixture in tortilla, roll it up, and place seam side down in greased casserole dish. Cover with enchilada sauce. Top with cheese and bake for 45 minutes.

Slumgullion

Here is a quick and easy dinner that you can make in minutes. I have no idea where it got this creative name. When I was in college there was a family who would invite me over to lunch every Sunday after church. Dad Guar would tell me to invite my friends and then ask how many people were coming to lunch and what I would like served. Then he would run to the grocery store and cook a wonderful lunch for all of us. Their generosity and kindness helped my transition from home to college and formed a unique friendship. Slumgullion was one of his specialties.

—Suzanne—

1 pound ground beef

1 tablespoon butter

8 ounces sliced fresh mushrooms

1 teaspoon paprika

½ teaspoon pepper

1 large onion, chopped

1 teaspoon minced garlic

1 10½-ounce can cream of celery soup

1 cup water

16 ounces medium pasta shells, cooked and drained

1. Brown beef in large skillet over medium-high heat. Remove beef from skillet and set aside.
2. Add butter and mushrooms to skillet. Season with paprika and pepper. When mushrooms start to brown (about 2 minutes), add onion and garlic and cook until tender (about 9–11 minutes). Return beef to pan and add remaining ingredients. Heat through and serve.

Daddy's Spaghetti

I think I watched my daddy make spaghetti over a hundred times. I do not have an exact recipe written down—Daddy never measured anything—but I have listed the basic ingredients that he used. I think this is as close to his spaghetti as I can get, and his was delicious. Daddy ate in New York Italian restaurants a lot while he lived in New York City and New Jersey.

—Martha—

2 pounds ground beef	2 or 3 28-ounce cans diced tomatoes	1 teaspoon salt
3 tablespoons olive oil	1 bay leaf	1 teaspoon oregano
3 medium onions, diced	¼ teaspoon garlic powder	2 4-ounce cans mushrooms
2 bell peppers, diced	1 teaspoon parsley flakes	½ teaspoon celery salt
3 cloves garlic pressed	2 cubes beef bouillon	1 16-ounce package spaghetti
4 6-ounce cans tomato paste	2 teaspoons Italian seasoning	Parmesan cheese

1. In a large stockpot, brown ground beef in olive oil. Add onions, peppers, and garlic, and cook just until onions start to get translucent, approximately 9–11 minutes.
2. Add the remaining ingredients, except spaghetti and cheese, and cook over very low heat, stirring frequently, at least 45 minutes.
3. Cook spaghetti according to package directions. Drain and top with sauce and Parmesan cheese on top.

We know what real love is because Jesus gave up his life for us. So we also ought to give up our lives for our brothers and sisters. If someone has enough money to live well and sees a brother or sister in need but shows no compassion—how can God's love be in that person? Dear children, let's not merely say that we love each other; let us show the truth by our actions.

—1 JOHN 3:16–18

Quick and Easy Barbecued Pork Chops

Quick and Easy Barbecued Pork Chops

I am always looking for a quick and easy dinner for my family. These pork chops are just the thing. All you need to do to round out the meal is heat up some green beans and cook a pot of rice. Presto—dinner is served!

—Suzanne—

4 bone-in pork loin chops

2 teaspoons canola oil

1 bell pepper, chopped

⅔ cup chopped celery

⅓ cup chopped onion

1 cup ketchup

½ cup packed brown sugar

¼ cup chicken broth

2 tablespoons chili powder

1. In a large skillet over medium-high heat, brown pork chops in oil, about 3–5 minutes per side, then remove.
2. Add vegetables to skillet and cook until tender, then return pork chops to skillet.
3. Mix ketchup, sugar, broth, and chili powder. Pour over pork and vegetables and simmer for 30 minutes; be sure internal temperature of pork measures at least 145°F.

Slow Cooker Vegetarian Spaghetti Sauce

When we lived in Benin, meat was often very hard to come by. One meal we ate almost weekly was vegetarian spaghetti sauce with plenty of cheese on top. After a while, the kids preferred it to sauce with meat in it. Imagine coming through the door and smelling this slow-cooked spaghetti sauce that has been simmering all morning while you were gone. Yum!

—Suzanne—

2 teaspoons minced garlic

2 large onions, chopped

4 14-ounce cans diced Italian tomatoes

1 15-ounce can tomato sauce

1 12-ounce can tomato paste

3 teaspoons dried basil

2 teaspoons dried oregano

½ teaspoon crushed red pepper

1 teaspoon salt

Mix all ingredients in slow cooker and cook on high for 4–6 hours. Serve over spaghetti and top with cheese.

Aunt LaVerne's Spicy Spaghetti Sauce

Aunt LaVerne was a teacher who graciously came to Togo to help teach my children. She was from Oklahoma and liked her food to have some kick. She would often have our family over for dinner and cook this spicy spaghetti sauce that she served topped with sharp Cheddar cheese. This spaghetti sauce is unique because of the carrots and the hot pepper. It is probably a bit different from any you have tasted!

—Suzanne—

1 cup chopped onion	1 teaspoon salt	2 tablespoons tomato paste
4 teaspoons minced garlic	½ teaspoon red pepper	1 cup chopped carrot
¼ cup olive oil	¼ cup vinegar	½ cup chopped bell pepper
1 pound ground beef	1 28-ounce can diced tomatoes	
1 teaspoon black pepper	1 28-ounce can crushed tomatoes	

1. In a large skillet over medium heat, sauté onion and garlic in olive oil until onions get soft. Add ground beef, pepper, salt, and red pepper; cook until meat is browned.

2. Reduce heat to low and cook for 10 minutes. Add vinegar and cook 3–5 minutes.

3. Add tomatoes and paste. Bring to a boil, and add carrots and bell pepper. Cook over low heat for at least 1 hour or until all vegetables are tender.

Savory Dill Beef

In Togo, you usually bought meat in the market. You bought it by the kilo in chunks. It often came wrapped in a banana leaf or tied up in a black plastic bag. It definitely was not ground up and packaged in cellophane. As a result, I have a lot of really good recipes that work well with stew meat. The slow cooking tenderizes it, and the spices make it taste like a much more costly cut of meat.

—Suzanne—

2 pounds stew meat	4 tablespoons oil	¼ teaspoon oregano
1 teaspoon salt	2 cups water	¼ teaspoon dill weed
½ teaspoon black pepper	2 beef bouillon cubes	2 tablespoons Worcestershire sauce
8 ounces fresh sliced mushrooms	2 tablespoons tomato paste	3 tablespoons plain flour
1 large onion, sliced	1 teaspoon dry mustard	1 package egg noodles, cooked according to directions

1. Sprinkle beef with salt and pepper and set aside. In a skillet over medium heat, sauté mushrooms and onions in oil until golden (9–11 minutes). Set aside. Place meat in skillet and cook over medium-high heat until brown on all sides, approximately 2 minutes.

2. Add 1¾ cups water, bouillon cubes, tomato paste, mustard, oregano, dill weed, and Worcestershire sauce to skillet. Cover and let simmer for at least 1 hour or until meat is tender.

3. Mix flour and ¼ cup water. Slowly add to meat mixture and let cook until thick and bubbly. Serve over noodles.

Easy Swiss Steak with Onions and Peppers

My children used to love Swiss steak, and it is so easy to make. My mother usually fixed this at least once a week. I wish I could tell you why we called it Swiss steak, but I can't. If I remember correctly, Mama would pound the meat before cooking it in order to tenderize it.

—Martha—

1½–2 pounds round steak

4 tablespoons plain flour

1 package onion soup mix

1 large bell pepper, chopped coarsely

2 onions, cut into rings

1 15-ounce can tomato sauce

8 ounces water

1. Preheat oven to 350°F. Either leave steak whole or cut into bite-sized pieces. Sprinkle with salt and pepper and coat with flour. Place in a greased 9" x 13" pan.
2. Sprinkle onion soup mix on top, and then bell pepper. Place onion slices on top. In a small bowl, mix together tomato sauce and water. Pour over top of steak. Seal with foil. Bake for 2 hours.

Hearty Beef and Noodle Dinner

*This is the perfect dinner for a crisp fall night when you've been outside raking leaves.
You come in cold and hungry and pull this wonderful dinner out of the oven. While in
Togo we did not have leaves to rake in the fall, and when we returned to the
United States the falling leaves in Alabama became a wonderful treat.
It is amazing how we take things for granted that we miss
when we leave this country to live and work.*

—Suzanne—

1 8-ounce package egg noodles

1½ pounds lean ground beef

1 large onion, chopped

1 15-ounce can tomato sauce

1 teaspoon salt

½ teaspoon pepper

1 8-ounce package softened cream cheese

1 cup sour cream

1 cup small curd cottage cheese

¼ cup finely chopped bell pepper

¼ cup sliced green onions

¼ cup grated Parmesan cheese

1. Preheat oven to 350°F. Cook egg noodles according to package directions, drain, and set aside.
2. Brown beef and onion in a large skillet over medium-high heat. Stir in tomato sauce,
salt, and pepper. Reduce heat and simmer for 5 minutes.
3. In mixing bowl, beat cream cheese, sour cream, and cottage cheese until well blended. Stir in green
pepper, onions, and egg noodles. Place this mixture in bottom of greased 9" x 13" pan, and then top
with beef mixture. Sprinkle with Parmesan cheese and bake for 30–40 minutes or until bubbly.

Crock-Pot Hamburger Stew

This is a frequent Sunday dinner at our house. You can either start it Saturday night or early Sunday, and when you come home from church dinner is waiting. Being a one-pot meal means less cleanup, too. This is my father-in-law's favorite meal. Once we watched him almost singlehandedly consume the whole pot! I usually serve this with cheese biscuits and a green salad.

—Suzanne—

4–6 peeled potatoes, thickly sliced

Salt and pepper

1 cup mini carrots

3 sticks celery, cut up

1½ pounds lean hamburger, browned

2 onions, sliced

1 10½-ounce can tomato soup

1. Place potatoes in bottom of Crock-Pot. Salt and pepper thoroughly, then layer carrots, celery, hamburger, and onions. Salt and pepper again, and then pour the soup over the top of everything. Pour one can of water over; don't stir.
2. Cook for 4–6 hours on high or 8–12 hours on low.

Anything Goes Party Calzones

My kids absolutely love this. They think it is the best party food ever. It is incredibly easy for a sleepover or any kind of teen party. Everybody gets to make his/her own according to their tastes, and so they are as individual as the kids at your party. You can make it as easy as purchasing rolled-up pizza dough or frozen dough or as complicated as making your own from-scratch dough.

—Suzanne—

Bread dough
(**Note:** If using frozen bread dough, let it completely defrost before using)
Flour

Filling of your choice
(such as pizza sauce, pepperoni, ham, bacon, sausage, green onions, chicken, broccoli, olives, mushrooms, bell pepper, and Cheddar and mozzarella cheese)

1. Cut each bread dough loaf into 3 pieces. Let rest at least 15 minutes before you start rolling it out. Preheat oven to 425°F. Roll portions of dough on floured bread board into about 8" circles. Place each circle on a piece of aluminum foil and put the person's name on it.
2. Let each child place whatever fillings he or she wants inside; try to keep fillings on one half of the dough. A few of our favorites are chicken, bacon, green onion, cream cheese, and mozzarella; or lots of meat, pizza sauce, and cheese; or vegetarian with no sauce and lots of cheese and veggies.
3. After they are filled, fold them in half, seal shut, and bake for 15 minutes or until browned.

The one thing I ask of the Lord—the thing I seek most—is to live in the house of the Lord all the days of my life, delighting in the Lord's perfections and meditating in his Temple.

—PSALM 27:4

Crock-Pot Mushroom Round Steak

I love my Crock-Pot. One year we had three children on three different basketball teams and one child coaching younger kids. Trying to get at least one parent to all the games meant that no one was home to cook supper, and we had to eat in shifts. It is almost impossible to burn anything in the slow cooker, and dinner stays hot for as long as you need it to do so. Dinners like this help us to make it through sports seasons!

—Suzanne—

¾ cup plain flour

1 teaspoon salt

½ teaspoon pepper

1 teaspoon dried parsley

1 teaspoon paprika

2 or 2½ pounds boneless beef round steak

2 tablespoons oil

1 10½-ounce can French onion soup

1 4-ounce can mushrooms, drained

¾ cup water

½ cup ketchup

2 tablespoons Worcestershire sauce

2 tablespoons cornstarch

¼ cup cold water

16 ounces sour cream

1. Put flour and spices in resealable plastic bag and shake to mix. Cut beef into serving-size pieces and add to bag a few pieces at a time, shaking to coat.

2. In a skillet over medium heat, brown the beef in oil. Transfer meat to Crock-Pot.

3. In a medium bowl, mix the soup, mushrooms, ¾ cup water, ketchup, and Worcestershire sauce. Pour over meat. Cook on low for 8 hours or until meat is tender.

4. Remove beef from Crock-Pot. Pour cooking liquid into small saucepan. Whisk cornstarch and ¼ cup cold water until smooth and add to cooking liquid. Bring to a boil and cook until thick. Put both meat and liquid back in slow cooker and add sour cream. Heat on low for a few minutes and serve.

Country-Fried Steak

This is one of my kids' favorite meals when served with mashed potatoes, green beans, and gravy. I have to watch my husband, or he will sneak into the kitchen and get one as a pre-dinner snack while I have my back turned!

—Suzanne—

1 cup flour

1 teaspoon salt

½ teaspoon pepper

1 egg

½ cup oil

2 pounds cubed steak

Gravy (optional)

Fresh cracked black pepper for garnish (optional)

1. In a medium bowl, mix together flour, salt, and pepper. In a separate bowl, beat egg.
2. Heat oil in skillet on high heat. Dip steak in egg, then dredge in flour. Repeat. Cook for 2–3 minutes per side, then cover and reduce heat to medium. Cook 8–10 more minutes until tender. Remove from skillet, garnish with gravy and black pepper if desired, and serve.

Country-Fried Steak with Yummy Mashed Potatoes (see Chapter 2)

Togolese Beef Kabobs and Couscous

There may not be any McDonald's along the road in Togo, but at every taxi stop there are men standing around selling kabobs or meat on a stick. It smells wonderful—smoky and spicy. Occasionally we would purchase some through the car window on a long drive, but up close it wasn't quite so appetizing. You might have an ear or part of the intestines or any other scrap piece of meat on your kabob. Definitely not good! Instead of street kabobs, we learned to make our own. This recipe works very well with stew meat or other tough cuts of meat. If you have tender steak cut up, you can skip the slow-simmering stage.

—Suzanne—

2 cups plus ¼ cup water	1 6-ounce can tomato paste	1 onion, cut in chunks
1 box couscous	½ teaspoon cayenne pepper	Fresh pineapple, cut in chunks
1½ pounds stew meat	1 beef bouillon cube	Skewers
¼ cup oil	1 clove garlic, sliced	
1 large finely chopped onion	1 bell pepper, cut in chunks	

1. In a small saucepan with a lid, bring 2 cups water to a boil. Add couscous, cover, and set aside. After 5 minutes, fluff couscous with a fork.

2. In a skillet over medium-high heat, add beef and 2 tablespoons oil; cook until beef is browned on all sides. Add ¼ cup water and simmer until tender. Remove meat from skillet and set aside.

3. Add chopped onion and remaining oil to skillet over medium heat and sauté until brown. Add tomato paste, pepper, bouillon cube, and garlic. Simmer about 5 minutes, and then put meat back in sauce and simmer 15 minutes longer. Let cool so you can handle meat.

4. On skewers, layer meat, bell pepper, onion, and pineapple. Brown them on grill. Serve with remaining sauce over the couscous.

Grilled Marinated Pork Chops

One thing we all enjoyed doing in Togo was cooking on the grill. Because we almost always lived in a house with a flat concrete roof with stairs leading to it, John usually built a thatch shade structure where we would often grill and eat while watching the sunset.

—Suzanne—

½ cup soy sauce

2 tablespoons brown sugar

2 tablespoons cooking oil

3 cloves garlic, minced

2 tablespoons lemon juice

4–6 pork chops

Mix all ingredients, except the pork chops, in a 1-gallon bag. Place pork chops in bag and marinate for 1 hour. Remove and cook on grill until internal temperature reaches at least 145°F.

Teriyaki Pork Chops

Sundays are hectic for our family. Being a preacher's wife means that your husband has to be at church early, and everyone in our family is involved in various areas of the church. This is an easy meal to fix the night before and put in the oven as I run out the door to church on Sunday morning.

—Suzanne—

½ cup oil

½ cup soy sauce

2 teaspoons sugar

1 pressed garlic clove

1 teaspoon ginger

4–6 pork chops

Preheat oven to 350°F. Mix all ingredients except pork chops. Place pork chops in baking or casserole dish and cover with marinade. Bake for 1 hour.

Quick and Easy Curry

As you can tell from this cookbook, my family loves international foods. My roommate in college was Indian, and she introduced me to all kinds of good food, from chapati bread to curry. This is a very easy and quick curry if you are a beginner or don't have much time to prepare it. You can serve it with a number of different curry toppings in little bowls on the table. Some good toppings to consider are almonds, raisins, coconut, and chutney.

—Suzanne—

1 pound beef or chicken

1 tablespoon curry powder

2 tablespoons oil

2 medium carrots, sliced

3 stalks celery, cut into pieces

1 bell pepper, chopped in chunks

1 teaspoon salt

¼ teaspoon red pepper

1 8-ounce can tomato sauce

½ cup milk

2 tablespoons cornstarch

Prepared rice

1. In a saucepan over medium-high heat, add beef (or chicken), curry powder, and oil; sauté until meat is browned.

2. Add enough water to cover, then add vegetables, salt, and pepper. Simmer for 45 minutes.

3. In a medium bowl, whisk together the tomato sauce, milk, and cornstarch, and add to stew. Cook for another 15 minutes. Serve over rice.

El Grande Mexican Beef and Rice Casserole

Grande means "big," and this is a big casserole. It is our son Chris's favorite, and our family can polish the whole thing off at one sitting. The yellow rice gives it a unique and spicy taste, but it is still mild enough that my little one likes it as well.

—Suzanne—

2 pounds ground beef

2 packages chili mix

2 28-ounce cans crushed tomatoes

1 10½-ounce can Campbell's Fiesta Nacho Cheese soup

½ cup milk

2 cups grated cheese

1 10-ounce package prepared yellow spicy rice

Crushed Fritos

½ cup green onions, sliced

1. Preheat oven to 350°F. In a medium saucepan over medium-high heat, brown ground beef.
2. Add chili mix and tomatoes, reduce to a simmer, and cook for 5 minutes.
3. In a microwavable bowl, mix cheese soup and milk, and microwave on high for 1 minute.
4. In 9" x 13" pan, layer half of the ground beef mixture, add all of rice on top of it, then add the rest of the ground beef mixture. Pour cheese soup over top, then sprinkle with crushed Fritos, grated cheese, and green onions. Bake for 20 minutes or until cheese is melted and bubbly.

Beef and Cabbage Stir-Fry

I didn't think I was a cabbage fan because I don't eat much plain cooked cabbage, but when looked at how much I cooked with it, I realized that I actually consume a good deal of this very healthy vegetable. You are going to love this recipe because it gives you meals for two days! Be sure and look at the recipe that follows (Beef and Cabbage Stir-Fry Calzones) to see what you do with the stir-fry on the second day for a totally different twist on leftovers.

—Suzanne—

1 cup beef broth	2 teaspoons sesame oil	1 tablespoon cornstarch
¼ cup soy sauce	1 tablespoon sesame seeds	1 tablespoon cooking oil
2 tablespoons rice vinegar	¼ teaspoon cayenne pepper	1 16-ounce bag coleslaw mix
3 cloves garlic, minced	1½ pounds steak, cut into strips (easiest to do if it isn't completely defrosted)	1 cup bias-cut green onions
1 tablespoon brown sugar		

1. In large resealable bag, mix broth, soy sauce, vinegar, garlic, sugar, sesame oil, sesame seeds, and cayenne pepper. Add beef and marinate in refrigerator for 2 hours.
2. Drain meat and save marinade. Stir cornstarch into marinade and set aside.
3. Add cooking oil to wok or large skillet on high heat. Add half the coleslaw mix and green onions at a time to wok and cook until tender crisp; remove from wok. Repeat with remainder of coleslaw and onions.
4. Stir-fry beef in wok in small batches until cooked to desired doneness. Add marinade and cook until thick and bubbly. To serve, place cooked white rice on platter. Top with cabbage mixture and spoon beef and sauce over the top.

Beef and Cabbage Stir-Fry Calzones

This is the ultimate recipe for using stir-fry leftovers. It is hot and tasty and different enough from the previous night's dinner that your family won't realize they are eating leftovers!

—Suzanne—

Stir-fry leftovers from Beef and Cabbage Stir-Fry

2 tablespoons sweet-and-sour sauce

2 10-ounce packages refrigerated pizza dough

1 cup shredded mozzarella cheese

1 beaten egg

Poppy seeds or sesame seeds

1. Preheat oven to 425°F. Mix stir-fry leftovers and sweet-and-sour sauce and set aside.
2. Roll pizza dough into a large rectangle. Cut into 5" squares (should be 10 squares in total). In the middle of each square, put 1 heaping tablespoon of stir-fry mixture. Add 1½ tablespoons cheese. Paint around edges with egg. Fold over and seal shut.
3. Place on greased cookie sheet. Paint tops of calzones with egg. Sprinkle with seeds. Cook until tops are lightly browned, approximately 20–30 minutes.

Choose a good reputation over great riches; being held in high esteem is better than silver or gold.

—PROVERBS 22:1

Cabbage Bundles

These were a surprising hit with my family. Mom Pullen asked me to try them out, and I made them. The kids had serious doubts, but after the first bite they gobbled them up. We all absolutely loved them. I think the secret is the bacon grease! Don't forget that we are southern and occasionally use a little bacon grease!
Just occasionally.

—Suzanne—

1 large head cabbage

1 onion, finely chopped

2 tablespoons bacon drippings

1 pound hamburger

1 cup prepared rice

1 teaspoon salt

1 teaspoon pepper

1 teaspoon paprika

2 8-ounce cans tomato sauce

½ cup sour cream

1. Preheat oven to 350°F. Remove large outer leaves from cabbage and cook in boiling salted water, about 5 minutes. Drain and cool completely.
2. In a skillet over medium-high heat, add onion and bacon drippings, and sauté until onions are brown. Add meat, cooked rice, and seasonings, and cook until meat is browned.
3. Put 1 tablespoon of the mixture on the stem end of a cabbage leaf, roll, and fasten with a toothpick. Place in baking dish and pour tomato sauce over the bundles. Bake for about 1 hour. Add sour cream right before serving.

Spicy Turkey or Beef Empanadas

I absolutely love this recipe. It is one more pie crust, but it is a phenomenal way to use leftover turkey, chicken, or roast beef. It doesn't taste like leftovers and has a lot of zip. As a missionary wife I always used all leftovers—absolutely all. Nothing was ever thrown away that could be used in another way in another dish.

—Suzanne—

2 pie shells unbaked (regular size not deep dish)
Note: The rolled-up crusts work better than those frozen ones that come already in pie plates.

2 cups prepared yellow rice

1 cup chopped turkey, beef, or chicken

1 cup shredded pepper jack cheese

½ cup sliced green onions

1 2¼-ounce can sliced black olives, drained

1 envelope fajita seasoning

2 tablespoons cornmeal

Sour cream

Taco sauce

1. Preheat oven to 400°F. Flatten out pie crusts.
2. In a medium bowl, combine rice, meat, cheese, onions, olives, and fajita seasoning. Spoon half of the mixture onto each pie crust. Fold the crust over and crimp the edges with a fork.
3. Place on a baking sheet sprinkled with cornmeal. Bake 25 minutes. Cut in half and serve with sour cream and taco sauce.

Hamburger Beef Biscuit Roll-Ups

Hamburger Beef Biscuit Roll-Ups

I made this for my family many years ago when the boys were little. It is terribly easy to do and fun to serve. My Aunt Chris gave me this recipe. She probably used homemade biscuit dough, but Bisquick dough works if you are in a hurry.

—Martha—

½ pound ground beef

½ cup chopped onion

½ cup chopped bell pepper

1 teaspoon salt

½ teaspoon pepper

2 cups biscuit dough

Melted butter to brush on top

1. In a medium skillet over medium-high heat, add ground beef, onion, and bell pepper; cook until meat is browned. Add salt and pepper and set aside.
2. Make biscuit dough according to package directions, and roll into a rectangle about ½" thick. Spread the beef mixture on the biscuit dough. Roll up like a jelly roll. Chill for 1 hour.
3. Preheat oven to 350°F. Cut roll into 1½" slices and place on greased cookie sheet. Brush top with melted butter. Bake for 20–25 minutes.

Tamale Pie

This was one of the first recipes I ever cooked and adapted. It was something no one in my family had ever cooked, and they were very tolerant of my teenaged experiments. It took me several tries to realize that you really do have to stir the cornmeal into cold water or else you will have nothing but lumps! You can make it with leftover chili for the filling, or you can leave out the beans and use a bit more meat. I have also made it with stew meat instead of hamburger for a tasty option, and added a can of corn to the filling. It is a wonderful and easily adaptable recipe!

—Suzanne—

1½ pounds ground beef

1 large chopped onion

1 16-ounce can kidney beans

1 16-ounce can tomato sauce

1 teaspoon chili powder

½ teaspoon salt

½ teaspoon pepper

5 cups water, divided

1 cup plain cornmeal

Shredded Cheddar cheese

1. Preheat oven to 350°F. In a saucepan over medium-high heat, add ground beef and onion and cook until meat is browned.
2. Add beans, tomato sauce, chili powder, salt, and pepper; cook until beans are heated through, approximately 5 minutes.
3. In a stockpot, bring 3 cups water to boil. In a medium bowl, mix 1 cup cornmeal and 2 cups cold water. Gently pour this into the boiling water. Stir constantly. Cook for 3–4 minutes or until thick and bubbly.
4. Pour half of cornmeal mixture into greased 2-quart casserole dish. Add meat mixture on top of cornmeal mixture. Pour remaining cornmeal mixture on top of meat mixture. Top with shredded cheese. Bake for 30 minutes.

Basic Sweet and Sour Pork

In Togo, we made a lot of different stir-fry dishes depending on what vegetables were in season. This is a very basic sweet-and-sour recipe that can be adjusted depending on what meats or vegetables you would like to use. Now that we're in the United States, I often just toss in a bag of frozen mixed stir-fry vegetables instead of chopping fresh vegetables.

—Suzanne—

3 tablespoons olive oil or other cooking oil

1 pound boneless pork loin

1 onion, chopped

1 bell pepper, chopped

2 carrots, sliced

½ cup water

2 tablespoons sugar

1 tablespoon soy sauce

2 tablespoons vinegar

2 tablespoons cornstarch

1. Cut pork into bite-sized pieces; in a skillet heat oil over medium-high heat, add pork and cook until browned on all sides. Add onion, bell pepper, and carrot, and stir-fry another 3 minutes.
2. In a medium bowl, whisk remaining ingredients together, and add to mixture in skillet. Cook, stirring constantly, until thick and bubbly.

South American Hash

I started making this dish many years ago. At first it looked a little peculiar to me with olives, raisins, and almonds in a hamburger dish. After serving it one time, my family loved it, and it became a family favorite. I might add that my boys were very adventurous eaters and not picky at all. They loved it when I tried unusual things.

—Martha—

2 tablespoons oil

½ cup diced bell pepper

¼ cup diced onions

1 4-ounce can mushrooms

1 pound ground beef

1 20-ounce can crushed tomatoes with juice

¼ cup sliced green olives

¼ cup seedless raisins

¼ cup slivered almonds

1 teaspoon salt

⅛ teaspoon pepper

Prepared white or yellow rice

A dash of other seasonings that your family likes (such as garlic powder, Mrs. Dash, Jane's Krazy Mixed-Up Seasonings, or Cajun seasonings—after you taste the basic recipe)

1. Heat oil in Dutch oven over medium heat. Add green pepper, onions, and mushrooms. Sauté until onions are golden, stirring occasionally.

2. Add meat and cook over medium heat, stirring constantly until brown.

3. Add tomatoes, olives, raisins, almonds, salt, and pepper. Cover and simmer gently for about 20 minutes. After about 10 minutes, taste and correct seasoning.

4. Add the other favorite family seasonings when you see how seasoned the hash is already. I usually doctor up all of my hamburger dishes with my family's favorites. Serve over white or yellow rice.

Roquefort Butter Fondue Sauce

How many of you remember the first fondue craze? You would fill the fondue pot with oil, heat it, and dip bits of meat into it to cook. I adored my fondue pot and always used it when company came. Actually, I thought it was the fanciest type of dinner I could make. I had the sauces in little dishes for each person. If I remember correctly, I used stew meat because finances were very slim. It would be fabulous with truly nice steaks cut up into bite-sized pieces. If you are in the market for a fondue pot, please get a heavy one. Light ones do not hold the heat, and I think they are dangerous! Here are my fondue sauces for a beef fondue party. Enjoy!

—Martha—

2 ounces Roquefort or blue cheese

½ cup soft butter

2 teaspoons prepared mustard

1 garlic clove, crushed

Combine all ingredients. Whip, cover, and refrigerate for several hours to blend flavors. Let stand at room temperature for 1 hour before serving.

Oh, the joys of those who do not follow the advice of the wicked, or stand around with sinners, or join in with mockers. But they delight in the law of the Lord, meditating on it day and night. They are like trees planted along the riverbank, bearing fruit each season. Their leaves never wither, and they prosper in all they do.

—PSALM 1:1–3

Horseradish Fondue Sauce

Joe is very fond of horseradish. When we have fondue he always requests this dish; I'm pretty sure this is his favorite.

—Martha—

1½ cups sour cream

¼ cup mayonnaise

1½ tablespoons horseradish

Salt and pepper to taste

Combine all ingredients; refrigerate for several hours before serving.

Red Fondue Sauce

I am a big ketchup fan. Go figure—I'm Southern. So I always have this "red" sauce, which not only adds color but gives me the ketchup touch for the beef. I made this sauce up when I first started "doing fondue" and found it to be good and inexpensive.

—Martha—

¾ cup ketchup

2 tablespoons vinegar

1 teaspoon horseradish

Mix all ingredients together well. Chill before serving.

Garlic Fondue Sauce

Garlic and soy sauce are terrific together, and mixed with mayonnaise they are superb. My children are all Chinese food fans, and this sauce is their favorite.

—Martha—

½ cup mayonnaise

3 cloves garlic, crushed

Soy sauce to taste

Combine all ingredients.
Chill before serving.

Caper Butter Fondue Sauce

As a child growing up in the South, I was considered quite sophisticated when friends found a bottle of capers in our refrigerator as almost no one had ever heard of this ingredient. I have always loved capers, so when I became a "fondue cook" I just had to find a way to mix something up using them. "What could be better than butter?" I reasoned, and it is quite good.

—Martha—

½ cup soft butter

3 tablespoons capers with liquid

Place butter and capers with liquid in small bowl
in mixer. Beat until light and fluffy.
Chill, then let it sit at room temperature
for 1 hour before serving.

SECRET SPAGHETTI

—Martha—

Love prospers when a fault is forgiven, but dwelling on it separates close friends.

—PROVERBS 17:9

When Mama and Daddy were first married, Daddy was an executive with G. Washington Foods in New York City. They entertained important clients at their beautiful home in Morristown, New Jersey, on Tuxedo Drive. Daddy was a wonderful cook and specialized in spaghetti. One night after appetizers, the guests were seated at the dining room table talking, and Daddy and Mama went into the kitchen to bring the spaghetti in on a gorgeous platter for Daddy to serve at the table. The platter was heavy and fully loaded. They had a butler's pantry between the kitchen and the dining room so one door had to be opened to go into the pantry, and a second door led to the dining room. Daddy never quite made it through the first door. He somehow lost his footing a little, and all of the spaghetti—enough for the entire dinner party— slipped right onto the kitchen floor. Mama and Daddy looked at each other, giggled silently, and carefully slipped that spaghetti back onto the huge platter, marched right into the dining room, and served the "secret spaghetti." No one even noticed, and everyone enjoyed the evening thoroughly. Mama and Daddy laughed about the Morristown dinner party nearly every time they made his famous spaghetti, and I guess it was a testament to how clean my Mama kept her kitchen floor.

Proverbs teaches us that there are two different types of people out there—those who focus on the faults of others, and those who seek to cover them up. Daddy was one of those wonderful people whose tendency was to cover up for others and focus on their positives. I never heard him say one unkind word about another person. He always said, "If you can't say something nice, don't say anything at all." Just like he was willing to cover over the spaghetti slippage, he was always willing to look for the best in anyone and cover up their minor flaws. I want to be more like he was and always focus on the positives in everyone I meet.

Tell Your Story

1. Have you ever had to cover a kitchen goof? Did you tell your guests or keep it to yourself? _____

_____

2. List something positive that you admire about the significant people in your life. They will love finding this tribute to them in your book! _____

_____

MY DADDY: FATHER OF ALL INSTANT BOUILLONS AND SEASONINGS

—Martha—

Do to others whatever you would like them to do to you. This is the essence of all that is taught in the law and the prophets.

—MATTHEW 7:12

My father, Paul Jones Campbell, invented the first instant bouillon in his kitchen in 1937. He also lived by the Golden Rule (Matthew 7:12). He was an employee of the G. Washington Coffee Company at the time. Daddy never bragged or talked about his accomplishments, but I thought you would love knowing that he indeed is the "father of all instant bouillons and seasonings." I copied the history of this seasoning and broth from the Homestat Farms website, with their permission (*www.homestatfarm.com*).

Here is the story as given on their website:

"In 1908, Mr. George Washington, a distant relative of General George Washington, established the G. Washington Coffee Refining Company, the pioneer of instant coffee, in Morris Plains, New Jersey.

Having successfully marketed instant coffee, the company was interested in developing additional products. In 1937, headquarter staff member, Paul J. Campbell, was served an exceptionally delicious dish while visiting friends. Impressed with the flavor, he complimented the hostess, who in turn showed him the seasonings she had used in its preparation.

Mr. Campbell discovered these seasonings mixed with water produced a pleasant meaty taste. His idea was to add dehydrated onion, celery, and other vegetables to the mix, in the hopes of creating an instant broth that could be sold as a companion to instant coffee.

Working late night hours and having tried numerous failed experiments with the ingredients, Mr. Campbell awoke one night at 3 A.M. having had a dream in which he made certain changes that produced a successful formula. Going to his kitchen, he recalled the changes made in his dream thus creating today's recipe for the broth . . .

During World War II, G. Washington's Seasoning and Broth was packed in "K" rations for the Armed Forces, replacing bouillon paste. Today it is recognized as the first of the Instant Seasoning and Broths."

To let you know a little further about the kind of family I grew up in, Daddy gave this recipe to the company during very hard economic times. Mama always said that with this new product's being sold to the armed forces, the company was able to stay in business. Daddy never asked for an extra dime. He never told this story publicly, though to have invented instant broth or bouillon was an incredible accomplishment. It was just part of his job as an honorable employee to help the company out in very difficult times.

Telling Your Stories

1. Can you think about something that truly stands out in your mind about your father? Describe how it impacted your life. _____

_____

2. Has your father ever cooked anything special for you and your family? Has your father ever invented a "new recipe" that only he could cook? Sometimes men love to invent recipes that need to be recorded. What was that recipe and what was the story that accompanied it? _____

_____

CHAPTER 4

Poultry, Fish, & Seafood

Since everything God created is good, we should not reject any of it but receive it with thanks.

—1 TIMOTHY 4:4

Original King Ranch Casserole

There are two versions of this delicious casserole. This one is the easiest.
The second one is this recipe completely redone for Togo since we didn't have access
to all the ingredients. My kids like the Togo version better than the version that calls
for canned soups, so even in the United States I usually cook the second one.
This one tastes very similar, but if you're short on time, it is the way to go!

—Suzanne—

1 10½-ounce can cream of chicken soup

1 10½-ounce can cream of mushroom soup

1 16-ounce can chicken broth

½ 10-ounce can Rotel Original Diced Tomatoes & Green Chiles, hot or mild

2 pounds chicken breasts, cooked and diced

2 cups grated cheese, any kind

10 tortillas, torn in pieces

1 onion, diced

1. Preheat oven to 350°F. In a medium bowl, mix together both of the soups, broth,
and tomatoes for sauce.

2. Place half of the chicken in the bottom of a greased 9" x 13" pan. Layer half the soup mixture, half the
tortillas, then half the cheese. Repeat the second layer in the same order, then bake for 1 hour.

Togo-Version King Ranch Casserole

Once in a while all the missionaries would get together for a cooking contest followed by a potluck with all the entries. One year I actually won the main dish contest cooking this recipe. Keep in mind that, in Togo, you would have to make everything from scratch, including tortillas, salsa, etc.

—Suzanne—

1 cup salsa

1 cup milk

1 teaspoon cumin

2 chicken bouillon cubes

2 tablespoons cornstarch

1 whole stewed chicken, diced, reserve broth

(**Note:** I have sometimes made this with smoked or rotisserie chicken and it gives it a really good flavor.)

12 tortillas

3 cups Cheddar cheese

1. Preheat oven to 350°F. In a saucepot, whisk salsa, milk, cumin, bouillon cubes, cornstarch, and 4 cups reserved broth. Cook until thick and bubbly.
2. Add chicken and tortillas and heat through, then pour into greased pan.
Top with cheese. Bake for 1 hour.

Potato-Chip-Coated Chicken Nuggets

I know, I know—who in the world makes homemade chicken nuggets in this day and age? Trust me on this—if you try this recipe, I think you'll be making them often. They are very easy to make and very addictive. My kids and I literally inhale them when they come out of the oven. The dipping sauce makes a large quantity, but it will keep in the fridge.

—Suzanne—

2 tablespoons milk

1 egg

2 cups crushed potato chips

6 chicken breast fillets, cut into cubes

1 stick butter, melted

1. Preheat oven to 425°F. Mix milk and egg in one bowl, and put chips in another.
2. Dip nuggets first in the egg mixture and then in the chips, and place on a greased cookie sheet.
3. Drizzle the nuggets with the butter and bake for 15 minutes or until golden brown. Dip in sauce.

Honey Mustard Dipping Sauce

My boys love honey mustard sauce on almost anything. When we had a fondue night at home they always wanted honey mustard sauce. I thought, "Why not put honey mustard on fondue?" They were very happy and that was always their favorite.

—Martha—

½ cup mayonnaise

3 tablespoons honey

2 tablespoons yellow mustard

1 tablespoon lemon juice

Whisk all ingredients together.
Cover and chill.

Oven-Fried Chicken

When John and I went to seminary in Columbia, South Carolina, we had a fellow church member who cooked the most amazing meals for huge groups all the time. She would cook up a batch of this chicken for thirty to forty people at the drop of a hat. Her hospitality encouraged us!

—Suzanne—

1½ teaspoons salt

2 teaspoons paprika

1 teaspoon celery salt

1 teaspoon onion salt

1 teaspoon pepper

1 teaspoon poultry seasoning

2 cups bread crumbs

1 chicken, cut up

1 cup milk

Nonstick cooking spray

1. Preheat oven to 400°F. Mix spices and bread crumbs in a 1-gallon resealable bag. Dip chicken pieces in milk and place in bag. Shake to coat.
2. Place on greased cookie sheet and spray with nonstick cooking spray. Bake for 45 minutes.

Coronation Curried Chicken

Lynne Holyoake is my dear sewing friend from Australia. Although this is not a Southern recipe, it is a fabulous recipe and has such a nice story. When I have visited Australia I have stayed not only at Lynne and David's gorgeous farm home but also at her mother's apartment in Sydney and at their apartment in Sydney. Lynne writes about this recipe, "This recipe was supposedly served at the Queen's Coronation in 1953. One of my sewing students has five daughters and served this chicken dish on the buffet table at their weddings. I often make a half quantity when I have chicken left over. It is very Moorish. I serve it with rice and salad."

—Martha—

2 tablespoons oil

2 medium white onions, chopped

2 tablespoons mild curry powder

¼ cup tomato sauce

2 tablespoons apricot jam

1 tablespoon mango chutney (available at gourmet shops and online)

½ cup mayonnaise

½ cup cream

2 cooked chickens, stripped of all meat

1. In a large saucepan, heat oil over medium heat, add chopped onions, cook for 2 minutes, then add curry powder and stir to combine.
2. Add tomato sauce, apricot jam, chutney, mayonnaise, and cream. Mix well, and add cooked chopped chicken. Cook until thoroughly heated.

Angela Jones's Chicken and Rice Casserole

My friend Angela will always have a special place in our family's life. During my pregnancy with Ben, I went into labor prematurely and our family returned to the United States to await his birth. I was on bed rest when she and her husband came and picked up our three older children. They took them to a small amusement park and played laser tag and all kinds of games with them. When people step in and are a blessing to your children, they always have a special spot in your heart! Angela brought us this fabulous chicken and rice casserole for dinner as she picked up our children. Later I asked her for the recipe and have used it many times.

—Suzanne—

1 10-ounce box Uncle Ben's Country Inn Chicken & Vegetable Rice

3 cups chopped cooked chicken

1 16-ounce can French-style green beans, drained

¾ cup onions, chopped

¾ cup mayonnaise

1 can artichoke hearts (chopped and drained)

1 4-ounce can chopped, drained mushrooms

1 10½-ounce can cream of celery soup

Salt and pepper to taste

1. Prepare rice according to package directions.
2. Preheat oven to 350°F. Combine all ingredients in large bowl and mix well. Pour in greased 9" x 13" casserole dish. Bake for 1 hour or until golden brown.

Chicken-Walnut-Olive Casserole

*I got this recipe in North Carolina during the two years I lived in Charlotte.
I loved fixing it for company and think it is quite unusual and very delicious.
In addition to being all of these things it is fast and easy.*

—Martha—

3 cups cooked rice

½ cup stuffed olives, chopped

½ cup English walnuts, broken

2 cups cooked chicken cut into large pieces

1 10½-ounce can cream of mushroom soup

1 cup chicken broth

½ cup cracker crumbs

1. Preheat oven to 350°F.
2. Combine rice, olives, and walnuts. Toss lightly. Place half of the mixture in a greased 1½-quart casserole.
3. Combine chicken and mushroom soup. Spoon half over the rice. Add remaining rice mixture. Top with remaining chicken mixture. Add broth.
4. Bake uncovered for 40 minutes. Sprinkle with cracker crumbs, and bake for 10 minutes longer until top is browned.

Fruited Chicken Salad

While we lived in Togo we often had to drive to bush churches over two hours away. The services lasted for several hours, and it made for a very long day. I would usually make either egg or chicken salad sandwiches and put them in a cooler with cold water. Then after church we would have a picnic along the way instead of waiting until we were home.

—Suzanne—

SALAD
3 cups diced, cooked chicken

¼ cup diced celery

¼ cup diced bell pepper

1 cup mandarin orange segments

1 9-ounce can pineapple chunks, drained, reserving 2 tablespoons juice

½ cup toasted, slivered almonds

DRESSING
2 tablespoons reserved pineapple juice

2 tablespoons oil

2 tablespoons wine vinegar

½ teaspoon salt

¼ cup mayonnaise

Mix together salad ingredients and set aside. Whisk together dressing ingredients and mix with salad. Chill at least 30 minutes before serving.

Poppy Seed Chicken

Poppy Seed Chicken

When we came back to the United States on furlough, we would travel and speak at various mission conferences. At the conferences, various individuals or classes would take on the project of keeping us fed while we were visiting their church. The first time I tasted this recipe was in Birmingham at one of those conferences. Different couples would bring us lunch at the mission house every day. When I tasted this chicken casserole, I knew I was back in the United States!

—Suzanne—

4 boneless skinless chicken breasts, boiled and diced

1 16-ounce package sour cream

1 10½-ounce can cream of chicken soup

2 tablespoons poppy seeds

1 sleeve Ritz Crackers, crushed

6 tablespoons butter, melted

1 cup grated Cheddar cheese

Prepared rice

1. Preheat oven to 350°F. Mix chicken, sour cream, soup, poppy seeds, crackers, and butter.
2. Pour into 9" x 9" greased baking dish. Top with Cheddar cheese. Bake for 45 minutes. Serve over hot rice.

Chicken Wiggle

My boys used to say that they wanted "mixed-up food" for supper when I asked them for their requests for the weekend. That meant a main dish in one pot or a casserole! Chicken Wiggle is a funny name for something that always pleased my boys.

—Martha—

1 large chicken

2 quarts water

1 stick butter

2 medium onions, diced

2 bell peppers, diced

1 4-ounce can mushrooms, chopped

1 2-ounce can pimentos, chopped

¼ cup Worcestershire sauce

1 tablespoon Tabasco sauce

1 16-ounce package egg noodles

1 16-ounce can English peas

Salt and pepper to taste

1. Cook chicken in 2 quarts of water until tender, approximately 1 hour, and chop in bite-sized pieces. Reserve broth.
2. In a large skillet over medium heat, add onions, pepper, mushrooms, pimentos, and butter; cook until tender. Add Worcestershire and Tabasco sauces.
3. Cook noodles in chicken broth for 10 minutes. Drain noodles and reserve broth. Add salt and pepper to noodles.
4. Mix together noodles, chicken, and vegetables in skillet. Add about 2 cups of the broth to it. Heat and enjoy.

Easy Chicken and Dressing with Cream Sauce

When John and I first went to Togo this was one of my staple recipes. We often had cornbread and black-eyed peas for lunch, and I would save the leftover cornbread to make this dish. We bought chickens live in the market. They were usually very tough. In fact, I have watched Togolese chickens kill and eat both mice and small snakes. They are tough old birds! I would usually stew them in the pressure cooker and tenderize them before making this dish.

—Suzanne—

1 chicken	¾ cup chopped onion	¾ cup plain flour
2 quarts water	1 cup chopped celery or bell pepper	4 cups chicken broth
1 8" pan cornbread	2 tablespoons margarine	2 cups milk

1. Cook chicken in 2 quarts of water until tender, approximately 1 hour. Remove chicken from heat and set aside. Make cornbread according to package directions.

2. Crumble cornbread into bottom of a greased 9" x 13" pan. Pull chicken into bite-sized pieces and layer on top of cornbread.

3. Preheat oven to 350°F. In a medium saucepan over medium heat, sauté onion and bell pepper in margarine.

4. In a medium bowl, whisk together flour, broth, and milk, then add to skillet. Cook and stir until thick and bubbly. Pour over top of chicken. Bake for 1 hour.

Maw's Fried Chicken

My grandmother never used a recipe to cook, and yet she was one of the best cooks I have ever known. Every summer, my brother and I would ride a Greyhound bus to Atlanta and spend a few weeks with my grandparents. When it was time to go home, Maw would fry up two whole chickens and pack them in a couple of shoe boxes just in case we got hungry on the bus ride. This is as close as I can get to her fried chicken. It works best in a cast-iron skillet.

—Suzanne—

2 chickens, cut up

2 cups plain flour

2 teaspoons salt

1 teaspoon pepper

1 teaspoon paprika

1 quart buttermilk

Oil for frying

1. Mix together flour, salt, pepper, and paprika, and put in a pie dish. In a medium bowl, add buttermilk. Dip chicken in buttermilk and then flour mixture; set aside. After dipping all the pieces, repeat the process by dipping each piece a second time in the buttermilk and flour.

2. Heat oil in a skillet over high heat, and add chicken. Oil needs to be hot (about 350°F), but be careful not to scorch it. Turn the chicken once or twice while cooking. Cook until crispy and brown on the outside and done in the middle (internal temperature of chicken should reach at least 165°F), approximately 24 minutes.

Paprika Mushroom Chicken

This is a creamy, colorful dish that is as pretty to look at as it is good to eat.
It provides a very warm and satisfying meal. As the mother of four young children,
I always love easy as well as economical recipes that all six of us enjoy eating.

—Suzanne—

1 large onion, diced

8 ounces fresh mushrooms, sliced

3 tablespoons oil

3 pounds chicken, cut up

1½ tablespoons paprika

1 large tomato, peeled and sliced

1 green pepper, sliced into rings

½ cup water

1 tablespoon salt

3 tablespoons sour cream

3 tablespoons whipping cream

1 package egg noodles

1. In a saucepan over medium heat, sauté onions and mushrooms in the oil. Add the chicken and paprika. Cover and cook for 10 minutes, turning occasionally.

2. Add tomato, green pepper, water, and salt. Cook on low for 45 minutes or until chicken is tender.

3. Cook noodles according to package directions. Just before serving, stir sour cream and whipping cream into chicken mixture. Serve over noodles.

Keo Paht

One of my favorite things about college was getting to be with other missionary kids from all over the world. This recipe from friends in Indonesia is simple and inexpensive to make.

—Suzanne—

¼ cup peanut oil

2 cloves garlic, mashed

1 medium onion, minced

1 cup chicken breast, diced

3–5 cups prepared day-old rice

1 egg, slightly beaten

Salt to taste

Fresh ground pepper to taste

Cayenne pepper to taste

1 tomato, cut in wedges

1. In a wok, heat oil over medium heat. Add garlic, onion, and chicken, and cook, stirring constantly, until the meat is white. Add rice and stir until it is hot and coated with oil.

2. Add beaten egg, and cook until egg is cooked throughout the rice. Season with salt, pepper, and cayenne, then add tomato wedges. Cover and cook 3 minutes longer.

Chicken and "Bikinis"

When our daughter Rebekah was tiny, the word "zucchini" gave her fits. She would call them "bikinis" because that was a more familiar word. So this chicken and zucchini recipe became chicken and bikinis.

—Suzanne—

3 medium carrots

2 medium zucchini

4 boneless, skinless chicken breasts, diced

1 tablespoon olive oil

¼ teaspoon black pepper

½ teaspoon salt

2 garlic cloves, minced

2 teaspoons freshly grated lemon peel

¾ cup chicken broth

1 tablespoon fresh parsley or cilantro

Prepared brown rice

Julienne carrots and zucchini. In a large saucepan, brown chicken in olive oil over medium-high heat. When it is almost done (about 4–6 minutes), add remaining ingredients, except rice, and simmer until vegetables are tender crisp. I usually serve it over brown rice.

Chicken Neapolitan

I love my electric skillet! Unless company is coming, mine stays on the counter all the time. I use it for quick quesadillas and grilled cheese sandwiches. For this recipe, using an electric skillet is best. It keeps everything from sticking and works really well.

—Suzanne—

8 boneless, skinless chicken breasts (small ones)

2 teaspoons salt

1 teaspoon pepper

3 tablespoons olive oil

1 cup chopped onion

4 teaspoons minced garlic

1 pound fresh mushrooms, quartered

2 10½-ounce cans Campbell's Tomato Bisque soup

¾ cup beef broth

1 teaspoon basil

1 teaspoon oregano

Prepared noodles or rice

Parsley or sliced olives (optional)

1. Season chicken with salt and pepper. In a skillet over medium-high heat, add oil and chicken breasts; cook for 8 minutes, and then turn chicken. Add onion, garlic, and mushrooms, and cook another 8 minutes.

2. In another bowl, whisk together the soup, broth, basil, and oregano. Pour over chicken, and simmer for 5–10 minutes. Serve over hot noodles or rice. Garnish with sliced olives and fresh parsley.

Mama's Famous
Sunday Barbecued Chicken

Mama always loved making this type of barbecued chicken. We had this on a lot of Sundays. She served it with rice and other fresh vegetables. In the winter, the vegetables were Le Sueur canned English peas and garden canned green beans (from my Nannie's summer canning basement). In the summer, we usually had fresh yellow squash and onions, boiled okra, and turnip greens.

—Martha—

Chicken pieces to equal two small fryers

1 12-ounce bottle ketchup

4 tablespoons Heinz 57 sauce

2 tablespoons mustard

2 tablespoons Worcestershire sauce

4 tablespoons sugar

¼ cup vinegar

1 package Lipton Recipe Secrets Onion Recipe Soup & Dip Mix

1. Preheat oven to 350°F. Bake chicken uncovered for about 40 minutes, or until tender. (Mama always cooked the chicken in a metal pan, although I'm sure a Pyrex or casserole dish can be used.)
2. While chicken is cooking, mix all the other ingredients in a medium bowl to make sauce. Cook sauce slowly in a saucepan pan on top of the stove over medium heat.
3. When the chicken is done, pour about half of the drippings from the chicken into the barbecue sauce. Discard the other half of drippings or freeze to use later. Pour sauce over the chicken. Cover with foil. Reduce heat to 300°F and bake for 30 minutes.

Joe's Birthday Crock-Pot Smothered Chicken

Many years ago I had to work all day on Joe's birthday, so I whipped together a Crock-Pot dish for the family party that night. Once I got home I had time to prepare rice, a salad, and broccoli, and, of course, my family's favorite, angel biscuits (see Chapter 1). I admit making a cake was a bit too ambitious, so I completed my meal with a birthday cake from our favorite bakery. Over the years this has always been one of my very favorite Crock-Pot recipes. Normally I cook 4 chicken breasts and use 1 can of cream of mushroom soup, but we had a large family gathering for the following recipe!

—Martha—

18 frozen chicken breasts

Your favorite chicken spices

4 10½-ounce cans mushroom soup

2 4-ounce cans mushrooms, drained

Prepared rice

Put the frozen chicken in the Crock-Pot. Shake on all of your favorite family spices. I use several of the salt-free ones as well as a little salt and pepper. I also add a few onion flakes. Spoon the mushroom soup on top of the chicken. Drain the mushrooms and add them on top of the clumps of mushroom soup. Cook on low 6–8 hours. It is tasty and has the most wonderful gravy to pour over the rice.

Parmesan Spinach Chicken and Pasta

One day I came home exhausted from speaking at a conference and found my daughter, Rebekah, and one of her best friends, Dominique, in the kitchen. They had set the table and cooked this wonderful meal for our family. They even washed the dishes! Thanks, girls!

—Suzanne—

1 16-ounce package spaghetti noodles

1 large onion, chopped

1 bell pepper, chopped

2 tablespoons garlic, chopped

4 fresh tomatoes, chopped

¼ cup olive oil

1 16-ounce can whole kernel corn, drained

1 8-ounce can tomato sauce

3 tablespoons fresh basil

¼ cup fresh parsley, chopped

1 bunch fresh spinach

2 cups fresh grated Parmesan cheese (1 cup canned)

4 chicken breasts, cooked and diced

1. Cook pasta according to package directions; drain.
2. Sauté onion, bell pepper, garlic, and tomatoes in olive oil for 10 minutes in a large saucepan over medium heat. Add corn, tomato sauce, basil, and parsley.
3. Stir in fresh spinach and pasta. Cook for 1 minute or until spinach wilts. Add 1 cup Parmesan and chicken and stir well. Top with remaining 1 cup Parmesan and serve.

Parmesan Spinach Chicken and Pasta

Scottsboro White Chicken Chili

What is more comforting on a rainy night than a creamy bowl of chicken chili?
I hope you enjoy this spicy treat. My sister Mary sent me this recipe.
I grew up in Scottsboro, Alabama, and Mary still lives there.

—Martha—

1 pound boneless, skinless chicken breast, cut into 1" pieces

1 medium onion, chopped

1½ teaspoons garlic, chopped

1 tablespoon oil

3 16-ounce cans Great Northern beans, rinsed and drained

1 14-ounce can chicken broth

2 4-ounce cans chopped green chilies

1 teaspoon salt

1 teaspoon ground cumin

1 teaspoon oregano

½ teaspoon pepper

¼ teaspoon cayenne pepper

1 cup sour cream

½ cup whipping cream

1. In a large saucepan over medium-high heat, sauté chicken, onion, and garlic in oil
until chicken is no longer pink.

2. Add beans, broth, chilies, and seasonings. Bring to a boil. Reduce heat;
simmer uncovered for at least 30 minutes (the longer the better).

3. Remove from heat, allow to cool slightly (to keep creams from curdling),
then stir in sour cream and whipping cream.

Tortilla Chicken and Dumplings

These are so easy, and the dumplings are the slick kind like Mama used to make.
In my family we did not like "fat dumplings" but "slick dumplings."
Mama used to carefully roll out her dumpling dough into very narrow strips
before putting them into the pan. She also liked them to be firm and not torn up
when they were done. These flour tortillas eliminate for me
all of the pastry stages of Mama's dumplings.

—Martha—

4 chicken breasts

1 14-ounce can fat-free chicken broth

1 14-ounce can low-fat cream of chicken soup

3 cups water (more if you like thinner dumplings)

6 fat-free flour tortillas

1. In a medium stockpot, add 4–6 cups water and the chicken breasts and boil until the chicken is done, about 15–20 minutes. Cool slightly, and pull apart into little pieces. Discard broth.

2. In the stockpot, add the fat-free broth, cream of chicken soup, and 3 cans water and heat over high heat until boiling.

3. Cut up tortillas and drop into boiling liquid. Simmer about 10 minutes. Add pulled chicken. Cook another 10 minutes.

Fat Chicken and Dumplings

*My mother always made fat white dumplings. They are almost exactly like
a biscuit cooked in chicken broth and are delicious!
They are well worth the effort!*

—Suzanne—

2 pounds chicken pieces

1 teaspoon salt

4–6 cups water

2 chicken bouillon cubes

2 cups flour

¼ cup oil

¾ cup milk

1. Add chicken, salt, water, and bouillon cubes to 4-quart covered saucepan, bring to boil,
   then simmer 15–20 minutes.
2. Remove chicken from broth and set broth aside. Cool chicken slightly, debone, and set aside.
3. In a medium bowl, add flour, oil, and milk, and combine into a dough. Roll out ½" thick and cut into
   wide strips. Bring broth to a boil again. Drop strips into boiling broth and cook about 15 minutes.
   Add chicken. Serve in a soup bowl.

Fat Chicken and Dumplings

Italian Chicken and Mushrooms

This is an incredibly tasty dish with a surprising ingredient—apple juice.
The fresh mushrooms make this dish; don't settle for canned ones.
I usually serve this with green beans and fresh pasta.

—Suzanne—

6 boneless, skinless chicken breasts	¼ teaspoon paprika	1 cup chicken broth
1 cup fat-free Italian salad dressing	½ teaspoon pepper	1 pound fresh mushrooms, sliced
1 tablespoon plain flour	2 tablespoons olive oil, divided	½ cup fresh parsley, minced
2 teaspoons Italian seasonings	1 tablespoon butter	
½ teaspoon garlic powder	¼ cup apple juice	

1. Put chicken breasts and salad dressing in resealable bag. Marinate overnight.

2. Preheat oven to 350°F. Discard marinade. Combine flour and spices. Sprinkle over both sides of chicken. In a large nonstick skillet, cook chicken over medium-high heat in 1 tablespoon oil and butter until brown on both sides, about 6–8 minutes per side. Transfer to a greased 9" x 13" dish.

3. Over medium-low heat, gradually add apple juice and broth to skillet, stirring to get browned bits off the bottom. Cook and stir for 2 minutes. Set aside.

4. In same skillet, sauté mushrooms in remaining 1 tablespoon oil. Stir sauce into mushrooms, and then pour over chicken.

5. Sprinkle with parsley and bake for 30 minutes.

The Lord says, "I will guide you along the best pathway for your life.
I will advise you and watch over you."

—PSALM 32:8

Southwestern Chicken and Rice

I love this cheesy chicken and rice. It is another one of those meals that is easy to make ahead and freeze. Every so often I buy a lot of ingredients and make multiples of several casseroles so I always have a stash of them in the freezer. That way, I can easily carry a meal to someone who is sick or pop one in the oven and set my magic oven timer so that my family will have a home-cooked evening meal on a night when I'm travelling.

—Suzanne—

4 cups cooked rice

2 quarts water

16 ounces chicken breasts

1 10½-ounce can cream of chicken soup

1 cup sour cream

1 onion, chopped

1 teaspoon chili powder

Salt and pepper

1 cup shredded cheese

1 15-ounce can diced tomatoes

1 14-ounce can Rotel Original Diced Tomatoes & Green Chilies, mild or hot

1. Preheat oven to 350°F. Layer rice in the bottom of a greased 9" x 13" baking dish.
2. Boil chicken in 2 quarts of water until tender, approximately 1 hour, and chop in bite-sized pieces. Put chicken on top of rice.
3. In a medium bowl, mix soup, sour cream, onion, chili powder, salt, and pepper, then pour over chicken. Layer shredded cheese over soup mixture, and top with tomatoes. Bake for 30 minutes.

Tangy Honey Lime Shrimp Wraps

These shrimp wraps are good either as an appetizer or a main lunch dish. When you bite into them you can imagine yourself sitting on a Caribbean island smelling the salty breeze and savoring the sounds of the steel drums playing. I have served these wraps as a snack while watching a football game with friends and family. They will disappear quickly, I assure you.

—Suzanne—

2 tablespoons honey

2 tablespoons soy sauce

1 lime, juiced

1 tablespoon olive oil

2 teaspoons sesame oil

1 cucumber, peeled and diced

1 pound cooked shrimp, peeled and tails removed

Salt

1 tablespoon toasted sesame seeds

1 head iceberg lettuce, cut into wedges

In a medium bowl, mix together honey, soy sauce, lime, olive oil, and sesame oil.
Add cucumber and shrimp and toss to coat. Season with salt and garnish with sesame seeds.
Serve the salad with the lettuce wedges to use as wraps.

Avery Island Deviled Shrimp

The Wilsons were a family in Togo who had a huge menagerie of all kinds of animals. Some of the animals were pets, while others were projects helping pastors develop businesses, raising and selling rabbits, goats, guinea pigs, etc., for income and food. Beth was our language and culture acquisition expert. She did our language testing and made sure we were happy and adjusting well. You always felt welcome and valued at their home. When we visited, this was the dinner she served us.

—Suzanne—

SHRIMP
1 egg, slightly beaten

¼ teaspoon salt

1 pound deveined, fresh shrimp

½ cup fine bread crumbs

¼ cup butter

4 cups prepared rice

DEVILED SHRIMP SAUCE
1 cup finely chopped onion

1 clove garlic, minced

2 tablespoons butter

1 10½-ounce can beef broth

2 tablespoons steak sauce

1½ teaspoons mustard

½ teaspoon Tabasco sauce

2 tablespoons lime juice

1. Mix together egg and salt. Roll shrimp in egg mixture and then in bread crumbs. Melt butter in skillet over medium heat, add shrimp, and sauté for about 10 minutes or until pink. Remove shrimp and arrange on bed of rice.

2. For sauce, sauté onion and garlic in butter in saucepan over medium heat until tender. Add remaining ingredients except lime juice. Bring to a boil and simmer 15 minutes. Add lime juice, and pour over shrimp and rice.

Joyful is the person who finds wisdom, the one who gains understanding. For wisdom is more profitable than silver, and her wages are better than gold. Wisdom is more precious than rubies; nothing you desire can compare with her.

—PROVERBS 3:13–15

Shrimp Creole

Shrimp Creole

Togo is a country on the coast of West Africa. In the capital city of Lome, many market ladies sell small heaps of shrimp for varying amounts. When we went to the capital, shrimp was a delicacy that we enjoyed.

—Suzanne—

1 stick margarine

1¼ cups chopped onion

3 cloves garlic, chopped

2 bell peppers, finely chopped

3 6-ounce cans tomato paste

3 bay leaves

3 teaspoons parsley

1½ teaspoons salt

1 teaspoon pepper

1½ pounds peeled and boiled shrimp

1 teaspoon paprika

4 cups prepared rice

1. Melt margarine in skillet over medium heat, and add onion, garlic, and bell pepper. Sauté until vegetables are tender.

2. Add tomato paste, bay leaves, parsley, salt, and pepper. Add water if vegetables look dry. Bring to a boil and cook 10 minutes, adding water as necessary.

3. Add cooked shrimp and paprika. Cook, covered, on medium heat for 5 minutes. Serve over hot rice.

Coconut Shrimp

When we first moved back to the United States, I flew to Colorado to see my brother. He went out of his way to make me feel at home and cooked some incredibly delicious food, including coconut shrimp, which I had never eaten. He is a terrific cook!

—Suzanne—

2 cups plain flour

2 cups cornstarch

6 teaspoons baking powder

1 teaspoon salt

¼ teaspoon Cajun seasoning

3 cups cold water

1 teaspoon canola oil

2 pounds uncooked large shrimp, peeled and deveined

4 cups flaked coconut

Additional oil for deep-fat frying

Mix flour, cornstarch, baking powder, salt, Cajun seasonings, water, and canola oil in bowl to make batter. Whisk until smooth. Dip shrimp first in batter and then roll in coconut. Deep-fry in hot oil about 2–4 minutes or until golden brown.

Grilled Catfish

When I was in middle school, my brother and I developed a passion for fishing.
We caught catfish on many fishing trips. In the South, we really like catfish
cooked almost every way.

—Suzanne—

6 catfish fillets

2 tablespoons canola oil

2 tablespoons white vinegar

1 teaspoon fresh lemon zest

1 tablespoon fresh lemon juice

1 tablespoon fresh basil, chopped (or 1 teaspoon dried)

1 tablespoon fresh dill, chopped (or 1 teaspoon dried)

1 teaspoon Dijon mustard

½ cup red onion, chopped

½ teaspoon salt

½ teaspoon fresh cracked black pepper

Nonstick cooking spray

Fresh parsley

Lemon wedges

1. Pat dry catfish fillets. Mix together oil, vinegar, lemon zest, lemon juice, basil, dill, mustard, onion, salt, and pepper in a resealable plastic bag. Add catfish. Marinate for 30 minutes.

2. Spray cold grill with nonstick spray. Heat grill. Remove catfish from marinade; reserve marinade. Cook fish on grill for 10 minutes or until it flakes easily.

3. Put leftover marinade in saucepan and boil for 3 minutes. Put fish on serving platter and pour marinade over top. Garnish with fresh parsley and lemon wedges.

Fish Fiesta

*I love this bright and colorful dish. The different vegetables make it as pretty
to look at as it is delicious to eat. Healthy and delicious is a good combination!
I first discovered this dish when I was following a famous and healthy diet program.
The whole family enjoyed it, and it has become a favorite. It takes almost no time
to prepare, which is another bonus.*

—Suzanne—

1 pound fish fillets

1 teaspoon salt

1 teaspoon pepper

1 small onion, thinly sliced

1 bell pepper, cut in rings

1 tomato, cut in rings

1 tablespoon snipped parsley

1 tablespoon vegetable oil

1 tablespoon lime juice

Preheat oven to 375°F. Arrange fish in greased (I use nonstick spray) 9" x 13" dish.
Sprinkle with salt and pepper. Top with onion, bell pepper, and tomato slices.
Sprinkle with parsley, vegetable oil, and lime juice. Cover and bake for 15 minutes.
Uncover and cook about 15 minutes longer or until fish flakes easily.

Mama's Tuna Casserole

Mama made lots of tuna casseroles. I don't think I knew until I was grown that tuna came any other way than in a can. Mama was a casserole queen; however, many Southern cooks love prepared casseroles. My children always thought they had a treat for a meal when it was "all mixed together." This casserole was a great way to get them to eat their peas.

—Martha—

2 tablespoons pimento

1 10½-ounce can cream of mushroom soup

½ cup milk

1 7-ounce can white tuna

1 cup green peas (cooked)

1¼ cups crushed potato chips

1. Preheat oven to 375°F. Cut pimento into small strips. In a medium bowl, combine soup and milk, and blend thoroughly. Add tuna, pimento, and peas; stir.
2. Pour into a 1-quart greased casserole dish. Sprinkle potato chips on top. Bake for 25 minutes.

Do not withhold good from those who deserve it when it's in your power to help them.

—PROVERBS 3:27

Glazed Salmon

My son Ben cannot seem to get it in his head that fish is not chicken. This is my favorite way to cook fish. Even in the middle of winter, I usually go outside and throw this on the grill. After all the effort to make a wonderful salmon dinner, Ben declares, "I want more of that good chicken!"

—Suzanne—

¼ cup honey

2 tablespoons soy sauce

2 tablespoons lime juice

1 tablespoon Dijon mustard

6 salmon fillets

Nonstick cooking spray

1 lemon slice for garnish (optional)

Fresh parsley for garnish (optional)

1. Preheat grill or oven to 425°F. In a bowl, mix together honey, soy sauce, lime juice, and mustard. If you are cooking salmon on the grill, first spray cold grill with nonstick spray.

2. After the grill is hot, lay salmon fillets on it and brush with glaze. Grill for 1–2 minutes, then brush with more glaze and grill 1–2 minutes. Turn fillets and grill 2–3 minutes, brushing with glaze several times. If baking in oven, brush salmon with glaze and bake for 15 minutes. Remove from oven, garnish with lemon and parsley if desired, and serve.

Glazed Salmon

Olive Salmon Casserole

Mama did wonders with canned salmon, mixing it into tasty casseroles and making salmon croquettes. I thought canned salmon was quite the delicacy, and it must have been common Southern fare. Joe's mother also served salmon croquettes often when he was a child. When I say I thought both tuna and salmon only came in cans, I am not kidding.

—Martha—

8 ounces shredded Cheddar cheese

½ cup milk

Salt and pepper to taste

1 cup prepared rice

1 7¾-ounce can salmon

½ cup stuffed green olives, chopped

1. Preheat oven to 350°F. In a medium saucepan or double boiler over medium heat, combine cheese and milk, stirring constantly. Add salt and pepper to taste. Cook until smooth, approximately 15–20 minutes.
2. In a 1½-quart greased casserole, place a layer of cooked rice, salmon, olives, and sauce. Repeat, making sure top layer is cheese. Bake for 30 minutes.

TRUE "WUV"

—Suzanne—

Pure and genuine religion in the sight of God the Father means caring for orphans and widows in their distress and refusing to let the world corrupt you.

—JAMES 1:27

Almost everyone in my generation has seen *The Princess Bride* at some point over the last twenty-five years. Do you remember the scene where the priest intones, "We are gathered here today to celebrate true wuv . . ." The good guy had sailed through dangerous seas, fought a champion swordsman, wrestled with a giant, even fought his way through the fiery bogs in pursuit of his one true love, Buttercup. My brother and I still tease each other with lines from that movie. Why the obsession? I think we all long for that true love. Recently at our Pulaski Pike campus (a part of our church that meets on a campus across town that serves underprivileged kids and adults), I saw an example of true love that far surpassed even fighting the swamp creatures. We had an evening Kid's Crusade and Vacation Bible School for the children in the Pulaski Pike area. John and I worked teaching the first graders. It's easy in the commotion to miss what the kids have to say, but one little boy politely raised his hand and quietly asked me if he could carry his sandwich home. How does that equate

to "true love?" Let me tell you . . . When we passed out the chicken sandwiches, his face lit up as if we had given him a priceless treasure, and he dug in, obviously hungry. Then suddenly he stopped himself and asked if he could take the rest of his sandwich home. He went on to tell me that his mom had told him that they didn't have anything to eat at home, and he wanted to give her the other half of his sandwich so she could have supper, too. A six-year-old child willingly forgoing part of his sandwich instead of eating his fill to be sure his mom had supper as well? That's my definition of true love!

The Bible teaches us that we are to care for the "widows and orphans" that are in our midst. I believe that covers single moms as well. It shouldn't be left up to a six-year-old to feed his mom. We should do all we can to share our food with others. That can be as simple as dropping off a few cans of food at a food drive or cooking a meal for someone who needs it. I might add that our church, Whitesburg Baptist Church, has a food pantry that serves many families in this area.

Tell Your Story

1. Write about a time when you were able to help someone less fortunate than you. This is not bragging but inspiring your children and grandchildren who will read about this and carry on your heritage of helping others. _____

_____

2. Describe how your church or synagogue has helped others through the years. _____

_____

_____

CHRISTMAS DINNER IN THE TOASTER OVEN

—Suzanne—

Better a dry crust eaten in peace than a house filled with feasting—and conflict.

—PROVERBS 17:1

I was a bride of less than two weeks when my husband declared we were going to have Christmas dinner in our own apartment instead of with our parents. I thought it sounded romantic. After all, we would be together. That was before I took a good look around our apartment. Our kitchen was a terribly empty room—it had a college mini-fridge, a hot plate, and a toaster oven. How in the world was I going to cook Christmas dinner in the toaster oven? We always had a big turkey and all the trimmings for Christmas. The first thing I realized was that I was definitely going to have to downsize everything! We needed to decorate but didn't really have the money for a tree. Then John gave me a beautiful poinsettia. The red flowers and green leaves were festive enough on their own, but since we had received some ornaments for wedding gifts, we hung them all around the poinsettia. It added a definite spark of holiday cheer to the drab apartment.

As I wandered the grocery store aisles looking for a turkey and dressing alternative, I spied some Cornish hens. Perfect! I bought them and the rest of the ingredients for my meal and headed home. I cannot begin to tell you what a wonderful time I had making that dinner. Because I could cook only one or two items at a time in the toaster oven, it took all day. I cooked stuffed Cornish hens, dressing, green beans, pumpkin pie, homemade rolls, and I can't recall what else. It was a wonderful, romantic evening spent with my handsome new husband.

That Christmas could have had an entirely different ending. I could have whined and complained and informed him that there was no way I was going to attempt to cook Christmas dinner in a tiny kitchen without appliances. I could have pouted and gone elsewhere for a fancier dinner. I'm glad I didn't. That first Christmas dinner eaten by candlelight on a folding table in a rundown apartment is a precious memory that I will always hold dear.

Keep short accounts. Don't let bitterness or a lack of forgiveness turn your feasts into a meal of sawdust. Instead, forgive and love the people God has placed in your life. It truly doesn't matter how much you have; love transforms any meal into a feast.

Tell Your Story

1. Write about the first holiday meal you made on your own. How old were you? Where were you living? What did you fix? _____

_____

2. How did you feel as you cooked your first holiday meal? Were you lonely or excited? Was it a happy time or a time of pain and physical separation from extended family? _____

_____

_____

CHAPTER 5

Appetizers & Party Foods

Everyone will share the story of your wonderful goodness;
they will sing with joy about your righteousness.

—PSALM 145:7

Martha's Parties

Most of my parties have been dental-related or engagement parties, debutant parties, or baby showers. In addition to the recipe dishes given here, I usually have a clear punch bowl filled with shrimp, roast pork tenderloin and rolls, a fresh vegetable tray, a fresh fruit bowl, and a dessert bar in the breakfast room. My most spectacular dish of the evening is always my Martha's Famous Showstopper Salmon Tray. It never fails to bring rave reviews. I always have a pitcher of ice water, and if I am giving a bridal or baby shower where I have a punch bowl, I always have a bowl of ice water "punch." That "recipe" is water plus an ice ring made in my bundt pan loaded with lemon slices and orange slices and other fruits if I happen to have them. Put these ideas together with the recipes in this section, and you'll have a Martha and Joe party!

Martha's Famous Showstopper Salmon Tray

Martha's Famous Showstopper Salmon Tray

I first made this salmon tray at Joanna's debutante presentation party. It was such a showstopper that everyone asked who had catered my party. When I answered that my family had done the party, no one believed me. This salmon tray has become a favorite of mine and, guess what? It is low calorie as well as very beautiful.

—Martha—

Pretty decorative lettuce, preferably the kind with dark and red leaves

One large tray—it can be silver or any other kind, but it must be large

1 cooked whole salmon (I purchase mine at Sam's in a package)

1 or 2 each of red, yellow, orange, and green peppers

Some of any of the following options: mayonnaise, mustard, caviar (optional if you don't like it), chopped onions (red are the prettiest), softened cream cheese, pimento cheese, capers, hard boiled eggs (quartered), anchovy paste, rolled anchovies, chopped fresh chives, sliced lemons, sliced cucumbers, fresh cracked black pepper, etc.

Crackers of your choice

Place the beautiful lettuce around the tray. Place the salmon in the center of the lettuce. Cut the peppers in half and hollow out the middles. Place them around the salmon like little bowls. Fill them with whichever fillings you chose. Serve with crackers.

Mama's Cheese Wafers

I have had very few parties where these have not been served. They are very easy to make and truly delicious. Joe's mother also made them for her bridge parties. She had both a Tuesday and a Wednesday bridge group. When she served these cheese wafers, she usually served homemade lemonade in her antique water glasses.

—Martha—

½ cup butter, softened

1 cup flour

1 teaspoon salt

½ teaspoon red pepper

¾ cup pecans, chopped

2 cups sharp Cheddar cheese, grated

1. In a medium bowl, beat butter until light and fluffy. Add flour, salt, pepper, pecans, and cheese, and mix together. Shape into 2 rolls. Roll each in wax paper; chill (preferably overnight).
2. Preheat oven to 450°F. Slice thin. Bake for about 10 minutes. Remove from cookie sheet and cool on racks.

Sausage Balls

I guess everyone in the world has this recipe, but it was the first appetizer that I ever made. Everyone loves them, so they're always a safe bet. Be careful not to brown them too much, and remove them from the cookie sheet immediately after taking out of the oven.

—Martha—

1 pound hot sausage

½ cup shredded sharp Cheddar cheese

2 cups Bisquick

1. Preheat oven to 350°F. Bring sausage and cheese to room temperature.
2. In a medium bowl, add Bisquick to sausage and mix well. Add cheese and mix.
3. Roll into 1" balls, and bake on a lightly greased cookie sheet until brown, approximately 20–25 minutes. These freeze well precooked, but let them thaw completely before cooking.

Olive Surprises

I adore these olive cheese balls. They are a little time-consuming but well worth the effort. They are so tasty that they will be among the most popular treats on your table. Be sure to make plenty, since most people won't be able to eat just one. I started making these right after I married Joe, and we started having dental groups from all over the country come to Huntsville for dental implant meetings. Someone always asked me for the recipe.

—Martha—

1 stick butter

½ pound sharp Cheddar cheese, grated

1½ cups flour

Dash garlic salt

½ teaspoon Tabasco

Smallest-size stuffed green olives

1. Preheat oven to 375°F. Using butter and cheese at room temperature, blend together with fingertips. Add flour gradually, blending well. Add garlic salt and Tabasco, and mix well.
2. Break off small pieces, flatten in the palm of your hand, and wrap completely around an olive. Roll this in your hand to be sure the dough is sealed.
3. Bake on cookie sheet for about 15 minutes. Do not overcook. These can be made ahead of time and frozen, unbaked. Let thaw before baking.

So let's not get tired of doing what is good. At just the right time we will reap a harvest of blessing if we don't give up.

—GALATIANS 6:9

Gouda Cheese Crescent Wrap

Several years ago my friend Patti Miller told me about this very easy appetizer.
It is well-received every time I serve it.

—Martha—

1 8-ounce package crescent rolls or puffed pastry

1 7-ounce round Gouda

1 egg, beaten

1. Preheat oven to 350°F. Separate dough into four rectangles, and press until seams of crescent rolls are gone. Wrap dough completely around Gouda cheese. Seal all of the edges and pinch to be sure all seams are sealed. If you are using crescent rolls, you need to pinch and pinch and roll and roll and pinch and pinch the dough again after wrapping it. If you do not, the cheese will run out!

2. Brush dough with beaten egg. Bake on cookie sheet for 18–22 minutes. Cool and cut into pie shapes.

Gouda Cheese Crescent Wrap

Beautiful Pineapple Centerpiece

Beautiful Pineapple Centerpiece

Having "showstoppers" on my party tables truly makes me happy. When the showstopper is as simple to make as this and also serves as food, I am especially pleased with myself. One year I had a party around the Fourth of July, and I used strawberries, blueberries, and marshmallows. Although the blueberries proved a little difficult to skewer on the toothpicks, it was beautiful.

—Martha—

1 pineapple

Toothpicks or shish kebab sticks

Cantaloupe balls

Watermelon balls

Strawberries

Pineapple chunks (canned)

Grapes

Cut off the bottom of a pineapple so it will sit flat. Leave the leafy top on.
Put a toothpick in the cantaloupe balls, watermelon balls, strawberries, pineapple chunks,
and grapes. Stick pierced fruit into the pineapple, arranging it in a pleasing manner
(make sure the toothpicks are hidden). Put several grapes on one toothpick.
Place remaining fruit around the silver tray.
It makes for a tasty conversation piece.

Pineapple Cheese Centerpiece

Follow the instructions for the Beautiful Pineapple Centerpiece, but simply put different types of cheese squares on toothpicks and serve. Using cheese rather than fruit gives you a different type of food to serve. It is just so much fun to have a conversation piece at a party. This takes a little bit of time, but it will receive rave reviews.

—Martha—

Marbled Cheddar cubes

Extra sharp Cheddar cubes

White Cheddar cubes

Colby jack cubes

Monterey jack cubes

Cut off the bottom of a pineapple so it will sit flat. Leave the leafy top on. Put a toothpick in each of the cheese cubes. Stick pierced cheese into the pineapple, arranging it in a pleasing manner. Put several pieces of cheese on one toothpick. Place extra cheese around the silver tray. It makes for a tasty conversation piece.

Share each other's burdens, and in this way obey the law of Christ.

—GALATIANS 6:2

Cheese Asparagus Crisps

These have been very popular whenever I have served them at family gatherings or at parties. You can refrigerate or freeze them; just be sure they thaw completely before you bake them. I have also made these with a jar of Kraft Old English Cheddar cheese rather than the grated cheese, and I have added minced garlic and a dash of Worcestershire. I think my favorite version is the one I have given, but you can let your imagination be your guide on the cheese mixture. I think the crusts on the white bread are easier to cut off when the bread is frozen; however, I have cut them off with bread at room temperature.

—Martha—

1 loaf white bread (square slices)

1 pound sharp Cheddar cheese, grated

2 tablespoons softened butter

2 tablespoons mayonnaise

½ teaspoon red pepper

Horseradish to taste

1 large bell pepper, chopped fine

1 can green or white asparagus

Toothpicks

1. Slice crusts off bread. In a medium bowl, mix grated cheese, butter, mayonnaise, red pepper, and horseradish. Add a little more softened butter if the mixture is not as spreadable as you would like it.

2. Thinly spread cheese mixture on bread slices; sprinkle with finely chopped bell pepper. Roll each slice of bread around asparagus stalks and fasten with toothpicks.

3. Toast under broiler until brown. Do not toast slowly because cheese will end up too melted. You can cut in half and use two toothpicks (one in each side) to make smaller rolls.

Alabama Caviar

This is a delicious dip for any party table. Years ago, I named it Alabama Caviar for fun, and it just stuck. Together with the Martha's Famous Showstopper Salmon Tray (see recipe in this chapter), the two dishes are real conversation starters.

—Martha—

4 cups cooked black-eyed peas

½ cup purple onion, diced

½ cup green onions, chopped

1 cup fresh tomatoes, diced

2 cloves fresh garlic, minced

1 medium jalapeño, seeded and diced

¾ cup vegetable oil

¼ cup vinegar

½ teaspoon dried basil

½ teaspoon pepper

½ teaspoon dried oregano

½ teaspoon salt

1. Drain and rinse peas; add to large bowl. Add onions, tomatoes, garlic, and jalapeño. Cover with the oil, vinegar, and seasonings, and mix thoroughly.
2. Refrigerate immediately and let marinate for at least 8 hours. Stir occasionally. Drain marinade and serve chilled.

Alabama Caviar

Hot Crab Dip

Joe and I have always enjoyed vacationing at the beach. A few times a year we drive down to Gulf Shores or Orange Beach and just enjoy being together away from everything. This dip reminds me of the good seafood restaurants that we enjoy at the shore. At every party that I have served this dip it receives rave reviews.

—Martha—

3 tablespoons margarine

1 small onion, chopped

½ bell pepper, chopped

½ pound Cheddar cheese, shredded

1 tablespoon Worcestershire sauce

4 tablespoons ketchup

¼ teaspoon cayenne pepper

1 6½-ounce can crabmeat

Chips, such as Fritos Brand Original or Scoops Corn Chips, for dipping

1. In a saucepan over medium heat, melt margarine, then add onion and bell pepper. Sauté for 2–3 minutes until onions start to brown.
2. Add cheese, Worcestershire, ketchup, cayenne pepper, and crabmeat, and stir until cheese melts.
3. Place in a chafing dish, and serve with Fritos or other crackers. (I prefer the Fritos Brand Scoops Corn Chips.)

Aunt Dot's Shrimp Mold

*My Aunt Dot Parks gave me this recipe many years ago. She and my Uncle Erskine,
a graduate of the Harvard Business School, entertained a lot since he was
a professor of business at the University of Mississippi. I started making this recipe
for parties about thirty-five years ago right after Joe and I married. It always
gets rave reviews. Be sure you purchase a fish mold to put it in. I have a copper one, but
any fish mold will do. Serve the shrimp mold on red and green lettuce leaves
for a picture-perfect presentation. This is so easy and your guests will love it.
By the way, it can be made several days in advance.
Refrigerate and cover securely.*

—Martha—

8 ounces cream cheese

1 cup mayonnaise

1½ envelopes Knox Original Gelatin

½ cup cold water

1 10½-ounce can Campbell's Cream of Shrimp soup

1 cup finely diced celery

½ medium onion, finely diced

Olives to embellish tray

1. In mixer, blend cream cheese and mayonnaise. In separate bowl, dissolve gelatin in water.
2. Heat soup (no water added) on a stove top until it is hot, approximately 3–5 minutes, and add gelatin while the soup is still hot. Add the soup and gelatin mixture, celery, and onion to the cream cheese mixture and stir to combine. Pour into fish mold. Refrigerate until set.
3. If using a circular mold, arrange olives in the center. The garnish adds a lovely touch, and the flavor blends well with the shrimp. If using a fish mold, arrange the olives around the fish. Serve with crackers.

Hot Pepper Jelly and Cream Cheese

This is so easy I almost did not put it in this section since it really isn't a recipe but an idea. However, it is easy and beautiful, and if your life is as busy as mine, you need exactly that—easy and beautiful! Sometimes I want to add a touch of color to my party table. Red or green pepper jelly is the perfect and easy way to do this. On Christmas day, our family comes over for Christmas dinner. I usually have this for them to munch on until everyone arrives for the big meal.

—Martha—

1 jar hot pepper jelly

8 ounces cream cheese

Pour pepper jelly over cream cheese. Serve with crackers. It's very pretty at Christmastime since the jelly usually comes in red or green.

Hot Artichoke Dip

I think my daughter-in-law, Sherry Ann Pullen, first introduced me to this hot artichoke dip. It is always served in a chafing dish at our parties so that it stays hot. We love it served with Fritos Scoops.

—Martha—

1 14-ounce can artichoke hearts, drained and chopped

1 cup mayonnaise

1 cup shredded Parmesan cheese

1 clove garlic, minced

1 bunch green onion stalks, white and green parts chopped (optional)

1. Preheat oven to 350°F. In a medium bowl, mix together all ingredients. Pour into a baking casserole or Pyrex dish.
2. Bake for 20–25 minutes or until lightly browned. Sprinkle with chopped green onions (tops and all) if desired. Serve with tortilla chips or crackers.

Spiced Pecans

*These delicious pecans are ones that Mama made a lot at Christmastime.
Since I usually have a dish of nuts for all of my parties, I serve them no matter what
the occasion. Another way of making delicious toasted pecans is to coat a quart of pecan
halves with ½ cup butter in a skillet. When they are coated, transfer them to a
300°F oven and bake about 15 minutes. Place on paper towel to drain, and salt.
Now you have two delicious ideas for sprucing up pecans when you want to
serve them in a special way.*

—Martha—

1 egg white

1 teaspoon cold water

1 pound pecan halves

½ cup sugar

¼ teaspoon salt

½ teaspoon cinnamon

1. Preheat oven to 225°F. In a small bowl, beat egg white and water until frothy;
add pecans and coat well.
2. Mix sugar, salt, and cinnamon in separate bowl. Add nuts and coat well.
Put into a buttered baking dish and bake for 1 hour. Stir often,
every 10–15 minutes, while baking.

*Who can find a virtuous and capable wife? She is more precious than rubies.
Her husband can trust her, and she will greatly enrich his life.*

—PROVERBS 31:10–11

Oyster Cracker Snacks

I dare you to eat just one handful of these! They are delicious and terribly easy to make. Plus, their little round shapes make them fun to serve. Set in small bowls around in the party area, they offer a great little snack on the same order as a bowl of delicious nuts. Now this is not a fancy dish at all, of course. It is just good. I might add that they are very inexpensive to make for a party or family gathering.

—Martha—

1 package dry ranch salad dressing mix

¾ cup salad oil

½ teaspoon lemon pepper

1½ teaspoons dill weed

½ teaspoon garlic powder

16 ounces plain oyster crackers

1. Preheat oven to 250°F. Combine ranch dressing mix and oil in a small bowl. Add remaining spices and whisk well. Pour over crackers and stir to coat.

2. Spread out on large cookie sheet. Bake for 15 minutes, stirring a couple of times.

Charm is deceptive, and beauty does not last; but a woman who fears the Lord will be greatly praised. Reward her for all she has done. Let her deeds publicly declare her praise.

—PROVERBS 31:30–31

Sweet and Sour Wieners

Kathy McMakin's special party food is usually these sweet and sour wieners. Oh, they are delicious and very easy. This gives you a meat dish with very little effort. We usually have sliced pork tenderloin with homemade rolls for one of our meat dishes. These wieners are usually next. You can also substitute meatballs in this recipe, and they are fabulous. Our "meat" course is usually rounded out with shrimp iced in a punch bowl. I'm sure at a fancy New York City party these would not be served. This is a Southern cookbook, and we do things a little differently here. This is a very inexpensive meat dish for a party. They taste so good.

—Martha—

1 10-ounce jar grape jelly

⅔ cup mustard

1 pound miniature wieners or cut hot dogs

Mix ingredients. Place into Crock-Pot or chafing dish, and heat to serve.

Party Pretzels

These pretzels look good and are perfect to serve at a party. Like many of our recipes, this mix is quick, simple, and delicious! My friend Judy first brought these chocolate treats for the dessert table at an engagement party that several couples were giving at our home. They were the rage of the evening for the dessert. When you discover how easy these treats are to make, I think you might want to try them. I warn you: Make plenty. Most people eat more than one.

—Martha—

1 bag Rolo Chewy Caramels in Milk Chocolate candies

1 bag square checkerboard pretzels

Pecans

1. Preheat oven to 400°F. Put 1 Rolo on top of each pretzel, bake until the chocolate turns shiny, about 60 seconds.
2. Take out of the oven, and top each candy-covered pretzel with a pecan. Press the pecan down to stick, but not so hard that you break the pretzel. Cool completely.

Emma's Party Chicken Balls

Joe's mother, Emma Pullen, always had these little chicken balls at her parties. Although she cooked her chicken breasts and diced the "real McCoy," you could certainly use canned chicken if you wanted to speed up this process. It is critical that you dice the chicken very finely. Please dice the chicken; don't mash it up. Mama and Joe's Mama, Emma, always insisted on having chicken diced finely for their chicken dishes as well as for chicken salad.

—Martha—

1 cup cooked chicken, finely diced

1 cup chopped pecans

1 tablespoon chopped onion

2 tablespoons pimento, chopped

½ cup mayonnaise

Dash hot pepper sauce

Mix all ingredients in a bowl. Cover and chill for 1 hour. Shape into balls using about 1 tablespoon of mixture per ball.

Be thankful in all circumstances, for this is God's will for you who belong to Christ Jesus.

—1 THESSALONIANS 5:18

Broccoli Dip

*My sister Mary is an excellent cook who entertains often and easily.
She never seems to get flustered over party preparations, and on top of this,
she worked full time as a social worker for most of her adult life. Now that
she is retired, I cannot imagine how many parties she will have and serve her
delicious broccoli dip and other party favorites.*

—Martha—

1 large onion, chopped

1 cup butter

2 rolls cheese, any flavor

2 10-ounce packages frozen chopped broccoli

1 8-ounce can mushrooms

2 10½-ounce cans cream of mushroom soup

1 4-ounce package slivered almonds

Salt and pepper

1. In a medium saucepan over medium heat, sauté onions in butter for about 9–11 minutes.
Add cheese; stir and mix until melted. Add remaining ingredients and cook until hot.

2. Pour into Crock-Pot and keep warm on low setting.

Bread Bowl
Spinach and Artichoke Dip

Putting anything in a hollowed-out bread bowl is a conversation starter. Spinach and artichokes are delicious together, and this dip is especially pretty when served in a large wheat bread bowl. You have probably figured out by now that I love conversation pieces on my party tables. I enjoy having people think that my table is creative, especially when my dishes are not very complicated.

—Martha—

1 package Hidden Valley Ranch Salad Dressing & Seasoning Mix

1 16-ounce carton sour cream

1 10-ounce package frozen chopped spinach

1 14-ounce can artichoke hearts

1 2-ounce jar chopped pimentos

1 large round loaf of bread, any variety

Assorted vegetables for dipping

1. In a medium bowl, add Hidden Valley mix and sour cream, and combine to mix well. Thaw and drain spinach well. Drain, rinse, and chop artichokes.
2. Add artichokes, spinach, and pimentos to ranch mixture. Cut top off of the round bread loaf and hollow out center of bread, leaving a 1" shell. Spoon dip into bread shell.

Bread Bowl Spinach and Artichoke Dip

GRADUATE-SCHOOL FOOD DAYS

—Martha—

Yet true godliness with contentment is itself great wealth.
After all, we brought nothing with us when we came into the
world, and we can't take anything with us when we leave it.
So if we have enough food and clothing, let us be content.

—1 TIMOTHY 6:6–8

When Camp and John were seven and eight years old, I decided to go back to graduate school full-time. I truly needed to get my Ph.D. finished so we would not have to decide on how many miles we could drive before our gas was gone. Although these were the first hard times I had ever known, they were very good for me and probably my children. In those days, paper towels and aluminum foil were the ultimate luxuries. We usually had some ice cream for dessert in the freezer, but it didn't last long. Our refrigerator in Northington Campus (student housing) did not have a very good freezer, so ice cream had to be eaten quickly. Occasionally, I would make Hamburger Helper and use one pound of hamburger meat for two meals. When I cooked a chicken, I would also divide it up for two meals.

The boys loved chicken and noodles, a meal that my grandmother fixed for them for a treat.

I have laughed at how much fun we had in this student housing. The facilities originally served as an army barracks, and my boys used to roller-skate up and down the long hallways. Northington had been a prison after World War II and even contained an old infirmary complete with antique medical tools. The infirmary had been deserted many, many years previously and was locked, but my boys and some of the other kids broke the locks and had a look inside. The barracks were used as student housing, even though they were condemned, and I had begged to be allowed to move into them during graduate school because they were the cheapest option. I was in charge of a Cub Scout troop during this time, and we used to dance up and down the halls. Since the buildings were scheduled for demolition, we were even allowed to write on the hallway walls. What great fun for an active group of Cub Scouts!

We did not have a lot of food during this time in our lives, but we made do, and the boys truly liked everything I served. I was quite thin in those days, and we never had extra money to run by a fast-food place or to go out for a meal. When I married Joe, I cannot tell you how much fun it was to go to the grocery store and buy really nice things to cook. I cooked about everything I knew how to cook that year and bought every spice and seasoning on the shelves. And I bought lots of paper towels and aluminum foil and plastic baggies. This was, of course, before the days of "green" shopping.

One of the true secrets to happiness is learning to be content in whatever situation you find yourself. My time spent in Northington Campus could have been spent in envy and bitterness over my financial situation. I could have worried and fumed over what I didn't have. Choosing to enjoy the positives, like being able to write on the walls with my boys, made those times into a cheerful memory instead of a time of pain. Learning to be content is a valuable life lesson.

Tell Your Story

1. Did you have to make some sacrifices to get where you are today? What everyday things are you especially thankful for because of that experience? _____

_____

_____

_____

2. What has been the most interesting place you have lived? What was different about it? _____

_____

_____

_____

WET SANDWICHES

—Martha—

Right now you have plenty and can help those who are in need. Later, they will have plenty and can share with you when you need it. In this way, things will be equal.

—2 CORINTHIANS 8:14

My guess would be that as you read the title of this section you were a bit disgusted. Who in the world would eat wet sandwiches? Quite honestly, I have left a sandwich on the plate if a dill pickle beside it dampened the bottom piece of bread with its juice. Years ago at one of our Schools of Art Fashion, we ordered sandwiches to be served for lunch. The plates were beautifully arranged with chips and a dill pickle. Unfortunately, the sandwiches were a little wet with pickle juice, and I sent them back. I won't even purchase a prewrapped sandwich in a stand at the airport for fear of wet bread. I want you to travel with me to Togo for a mission trip with John and Suzanne. Our team had worked with them for several days in the town of Kara, and it was time to drive to Lome and fly home. Suzanne had fixed lovely sandwiches for the seven-hour trip over very bumpy roads. I really dreaded the ride. The worst part of the drive was being stopped many times by soldiers

with guns at checkpoints who usually asked if we had something to give them. John always kept Christian tracts written in French in his glove compartment to give away.

There was only one gas station with a restroom on this desolate stretch of road filled with deep potholes. We made plans to stop for gas and eat our picnic lunch there. Suzanne had carefully frozen ice and put it in several bags to keep the lunch cold in the coolers. Somehow the ice had melted and leaked out making the sandwiches wet. Of course, we had other things for lunch, but we pampered Americans were not going to eat wet sandwiches.

I offered to gather up the sandwiches and take them to the nearest garbage can. Suzanne said, "No. Do you see those children over there? They will want them." She called them over to the car and gave the soggy sandwiches to them. They gobbled them down with great thanks. They never noticed that they were not "right." They were hungry and thankful to have anything to eat.

I need to remind myself that there are food needs here in Huntsville, Alabama, in addition to Africa. I need to be sure that I have personally contributed to the organizations, which are indeed providing food for those less fortunate. I need to constantly thank God for all of my family's food and to always remember in prayer those who do not have food for their families.

Looking at the verse at the beginning of this devotion, we can easily see that my abundance met their need. The children were hungry, and our abundance of food met a need in their lives. But their abundance meeting a need in my life seems a bit more complicated until I remember the lessons they taught me about having a thankful heart, not living a wasteful life, and enjoying all I have been given with gratitude. Even a soggy sandwich gains value when received with a joyful heart. Giving really does flow in both directions.

Tell Your Story

1. Have you ever met anyone who was genuinely hungry? Were you able to make a difference for him or her? _____

_____

_____

_____

_____

2. Tell about a close encounter with poverty that changed the way you have lived your life. _____

_____

_____

_____

_____

CHAPTER 6

Desserts

How sweet your words taste to me; they are sweeter than honey.

—PSALM 119:103

Italian Cream Cake

This is such a special Christmas cake since my family has always had a white cake at Christmas. This tradition started with my Grandmother Campbell who always made a coconut cake for Christmas. The white was to celebrate the birth of Christ. I never knew my Daddy's mother. Her father was a Methodist preacher, Reverend Dempsey William Ward, who came with thirty other Methodist ministers in 1870 to start the Alabama conference for the Methodist Church. He eventually served as a pastor for a church in Scottsboro, which is how my father's family became Scottsboro residents.

—Martha—

CAKE
1 stick butter

½ cup vegetable oil

2 cups sugar

5 eggs, separated

1 teaspoon baking soda

1 cup buttermilk

2 cups flour, sifted

1 teaspoon vanilla

1 cup shredded coconut

½ cup nuts, chopped

ICING
2 8-ounce packages cream cheese, softened

2 sticks butter, softened

2 teaspoons vanilla

2 16-ounce boxes powdered sugar

1 cup finely chopped pecans

1. Preheat oven to 325°F.
2. In a medium bowl or stand mixer, beat butter, oil, and sugar until sugar is combined and mixture is light and fluffy (butter should almost double in size and lighten in color). Add egg yolks one at a time, beating after each one.
3. In a small bowl, mix baking soda and buttermilk. Add flour to batter, alternating with buttermilk mixture. Add vanilla, coconut, and chopped nuts. Beat egg whites and fold into mixture.
4. Pour into a greased and floured 9" x 13" cake pan for a sheet cake or into three 8" or 9" round layer pans. (I always make three layers.) Bake for 45 minutes. Remove from heat and let cool.
5. For icing, beat cream cheese and butter. Add vanilla and powdered sugar; beat until thick. Stir in pecans.
6. Frost each layer of the cake with icing and serve.

Healthy Carrot Cake

This is a much healthier version of a traditional carrot cake. Using apple sauce eliminates the need for oil, and the whole-wheat flour gives the cake both a nutty taste and a fiber boost. My family loves desserts, of course, but I have tried to make some of them a little healthier. A friend gave me this recipe, and it is truly good. My family does not know the difference between an applesauce cake and one that has oil.

—Suzanne—

2 cups plain flour

1 cup whole-wheat flour

1 teaspoon baking soda

2 teaspoons baking powder

2 teaspoons cinnamon

1 cup sugar

4 eggs

1¼ cups applesauce

3 cups grated carrots

½ cup raisins

½ cup chopped walnuts

1. Preheat oven to 350°F. Sift together dry ingredients. In a separate medium bowl, add eggs, applesauce, carrots, raisins, and walnuts; stir to combine. Add dry ingredients; mix well.

2. Pour into two greased 9" round pans. Bake for 30–35 minutes. Cool and frost with cream cheese frosting.

Watergate Pistachio Pudding Cake

This light green cake with pecans and coconut makes a special addition to any holiday meal. How many of you remember the Watergate scandal? The evening news reported this event from 1972 until 1974 when President Nixon resigned. Wouldn't you know that a cake recipe would become all the rage during this time? This cake is delicious, and I might add that serving it to a younger generation might necessitate explaining Watergate.

—Martha—

CAKE	FROSTING
1 white cake mix	2 envelopes Dream Whip
3 eggs	1–1½ cups milk
1 3-ounce package instant pistachio pudding	½ cup pecans, chopped
1 cup oil	1 3-ounce package instant pistachio pudding
1 cup 7UP or lemon-lime soda	
½ cup pecans, chopped	
½ cup flaked coconut	

1. Preheat oven to 350°F. In a medium bowl, add cake mix, eggs, pudding, oil, soda, pecans, and coconut. Stir to combine.
2. Bake in 9" x 13" pan for 30–40 minutes. Cool completely before frosting.
3. In a medium bowl, add Dream Whip packets and milk; whip until stiff. Add dry pudding, stir to combine, and fold in pecans. Frost cake and refrigerate.

1-2-3-4 Cake

This is a good "missionary" cake. What is a missionary cake? It doesn't have many ingredients, so you can make it almost anywhere in the world. It is also a fun cake to make with your preschooler as you are teaching her/him how to count.

—Suzanne—

1 cup margarine, softened

2 cups sugar

3 cups flour

4 eggs

1 teaspoon baking powder

Pinch salt

1 cup milk

1 teaspoon vanilla

Preheat oven to 350°F. Mix together all ingredients. Pour into either a greased 9" x 13" pan or two greased 8" square pans. Bake for 30 minutes.

They are more desirable than gold, even the finest gold. They are sweeter than honey, even honey dripping from the comb.

—PSALM 19:10

Punch Bowl Cake

Place settings, other serving pieces, and decorations are as crucial to my holiday meals as the ingredients. Mama was like that, too. She loved china and silver and beautiful dishes. We shared that love, and because of it, I have way too many sets of gorgeous china. I also have my Mama's punch bowls—a large silver one she used when she made punch for church affairs, bridal showers, or events at the Scottsboro Heritage Center, and a small glass one she often used for desserts like this Punch Bowl Cake. She would call desserts like this one "showy." I guess she loved show business as much as I did since she and Daddy took us to Broadway plays every other year in New York.

—Martha—

1 box yellow cake mix

1 6-ounce box vanilla cook pudding

1 glass punch bowl

1 20-ounce can cherry pie filling

1 16-ounce carton whipped topping

1 20-ounce can crushed pineapple in heavy syrup, drained

1. Make cake according to package directions and bake. Cook pudding according to directions; cool.
2. Layer in the punch bowl in following order: Crumble a third of the cake in the bottom of the punch bowl. Spoon the cooked pudding over the cake. Spoon in the cherry pie filling. Spoon in the pineapple. Leave enough for two more layers of each. Spread whipped topping over the top.

Mississippi Mud Brownie Cake

Growing up, I loved going to Aunt Peggy's house. We spent many vacations with her, and before our arrival, she would spend days cooking all kinds of treats for us to enjoy while we stayed with her. This rich, decadent dessert has long been one of my favorites. Chocolate, nuts, marshmallows, and then more chocolate . . . you can't go wrong with that!

—Suzanne—

BROWNIE CAKE

2 sticks butter

½ cup cocoa

2 cups sugar

4 eggs, slightly beaten

1½ cups flour

Pinch of salt

1 cup chopped nuts

1 teaspoon vanilla

1 16-ounce bag miniature marshmallows to cover top

FROSTING

½ stick butter

1 pound powdered sugar

½ cup evaporated milk

⅓ cup cocoa

1. Preheat oven to 350°F. Melt butter in pan on stovetop. Stir in cocoa and remove from heat.
2. Pour mixture into mixing bowl and add sugar and eggs. Mix well. Add flour, salt, nuts, and vanilla; stir to combine.
3. Pour into greased 9" x 13" pan and bake for 35 minutes. Remove from oven and cover top of cake with marshmallows. Return to oven for 4 minutes to melt marshmallows.
4. Make frosting by melting butter, and then adding remaining ingredients. Mix well and drizzle over marshmallows. Serve warm with vanilla ice cream.

Basic Butter Cake

This is a moist, very buttery cake, which is ideal to serve at birthdays. When we were missionaries in Togo, I made it as the base for my daughter's sixth birthday cake. I wanted to make a carousel-like I had seen in a magazine, but Animal Crackers weren't readily available in Togo. That week our local store in northern Togo just "happened" to get a supply of animal cookies! I made a round cake, frosted the animal cookies to put on top (using straws for the poles), and then trimmed a paper plate to make a top for the carousel trimmed in ribbon. It was the cutest cake ever, and God had provided the animals we needed!

—Suzanne—

¾ cup butter, softened (1½ sticks)

1¼ cups sugar

2 cups plain flour

2 teaspoons baking powder

¼ teaspoon salt

¼ cup milk

1½ teaspoons vanilla

3 eggs

1. Preheat oven to 350°F. In a medium bowl, beat together butter and sugar until sugar is combined and mixture is light and fluffy (butter should almost double in size and lighten in color).
2. In a separate bowl, sift together flour, baking powder, and salt. In a small bowl, mix together milk and vanilla. Add eggs one at a time to butter and sugar mixture.
3. Alternate adding flour and milk mixtures to egg mixture until well blended. Pour into two greased 9" round pans or one 9" x 13" pan. Bake for 25–35 minutes depending on pan size.

Spice Cake with Maple and Caramel Frosting

This cake is beyond wonderful. I'm a chocolate fiend, and there isn't any chocolate in this, but it just tastes like Christmas. The spices in this very moist cake are wonderful, and when you top it with maple/caramel frosting it is positively addicting! This was a favorite Togo recipe. We always got a little homesick at Christmastime when we lived in Africa. This cake reminded us of home, and I always cooked it at Christmas, as well as at other times.

—Suzanne—

CAKE
2 cups flour

1 teaspoon cinnamon

½ teaspoon cloves

½ teaspoon allspice

¼ teaspoon nutmeg

½ teaspoon salt

1 teaspoon baking soda

2 teaspoons baking powder

2 eggs

1 cup sugar

2 tablespoons molasses

1 cup buttermilk

⅔ cup oil

FROSTING
½ cup butter

1 cup brown sugar

¼ cup milk

2 cups powdered sugar

1. Preheat oven to 375°F. For cake: Sift together flour, spices, baking soda, and baking powder, and set aside. Beat together the eggs, sugar, and molasses. Alternate adding the flour mixture and buttermilk to the egg mixture; stir well. When it is well blended, gently stir in the oil. Pour into a greased 9" x 13" pan. Bake for 25 minutes.

2. For frosting: In a medium saucepan, cook butter and brown sugar over low heat for 2 minutes. Stir constantly so it doesn't scorch. Add milk and continue to cook and stir until it boils. Remove from heat, cool, and add powdered sugar. Pour over cake.

Mrs. Perry's Pound Cake

How can something so simple taste so good? This is the pound cake that Mrs. Perry would labor to fix for our family when I was a child. Mrs. Perry was an elderly woman from my father's congregation who rarely left her house. She had a bedridden husband she cared for. Mrs. Perry prayed while she cooked. This cake always tasted so good to me that I think love was the secret ingredient.

—Suzanne—

1 cup butter

2 cups sugar

6 eggs

2 cups plain flour

2 teaspoons vanilla

Preheat oven to 300°F. It is important to prepare this recipe in the order instructed or the texture of the cake will change. In a medium bowl, beat together butter and sugar until sugar is combined and mixture is light and fluffy (butter should almost double in size and lighten in color). Add the eggs one at a time until well blended.
Slowly beat in the flour and vanilla. Bake in a greased tube pan 1 hour.

Give thanks to the Lord and proclaim his greatness. Let the whole world know what he has done. Sing to him; yes, sing his praises. Tell everyone about his wonderful deeds.

—1 CHRONICLES 16:8–9

Devil's Food Cake

Devil's Food Cake

This was the cake that my mom fixed most often. It is amazing how I remember this cake so often from my childhood. For almost every birthday, she would make this cake with a fluffy white frosting. I love making this cake for my family and love telling the stories about when Mom cooked it for me.

—Suzanne—

2½ cups plain flour

½ cup unsweetened cocoa

1½ teaspoons baking soda

1 teaspoon salt

1¾ cups sugar

2 sticks butter

3 eggs

1⅓ cups buttermilk

1½ teaspoons vanilla

1 batch Seven-Minute Frosting (see following recipe)

1. Preheat oven to 350°F. In a medium bowl, sift together flour, cocoa, baking soda, and salt. (Don't skip this step if you want a light, fluffy cake!) In a separate bowl, beat together sugar, vanilla, and butter until sugar is combined and mixture is light and fluffy (butter should almost double in size and lighten in color), then add eggs one at a time, beating after each addition.
2. Alternate pouring the flour mixture and buttermilk into the sugar and butter mixture until well blended. Pour into a greased 8" round or square pans and bake for 30 minutes. Frost with Seven-Minute Frosting and serve.

Seven-Minute Frosting

This recipe appears in nearly every Southern cookbook. My Mom made it quickly and easily, and you can, too.

—Suzanne—

2 egg whites

1½ cups sugar

Pinch salt

2 teaspoons light corn syrup

½ cup water

1 teaspoon vanilla

1. Add egg whites, sugar, salt, corn syrup, and water to the top of a double boiler and mix well. Make sure water in the bottom of the double boiler is boiling. Using a hand-held mixer, beat this mixture for about 7 minutes until it holds in peaks.

2. Remove the icing from the double boiler, add vanilla, and beat until the frosting is cool and will stand in firm peaks. This will probably take about another 6 minutes.

Sweet Potato Cake

In Togo, sweet potatoes grow in abundance during part of the year. This was a delicious way to make good use of them. In the South, we have always loved creative cooking with sweet potatoes. Many make sweet potato pie rather than pumpkin pie. Baked sweet potatoes have always been favorites in the South.

—Suzanne—

1 cup cold mashed sweet potatoes

⅓ cup shortening

⅓ cup water

1 egg

1⅔ cups all-purpose flour

1⅓ cups sugar

1 teaspoon salt

1 teaspoon ground cinnamon

1 teaspoon baking soda

¼ teaspoon baking powder

¼ teaspoon ground ginger

Preheat oven to 350°F. In a medium bowl, mix together all ingredients. Pour into a greased 11" x 7" pan. Bake 45 minutes to 1 hour.

Mama Randall's Chocolate Cake

This cake is named after the missionary who introduced me to it. She is a precious lady who "mothered" me for my first summer in Africa. At age nineteen, I had the opportunity to go to Zimbabwe for three months. Mama Randall cooked my meals and cared for me all summer long as I worked in the hospital and villages around Sanyati.

—Suzanne—

2 cups sugar

2 cups plain flour

½ teaspoon salt

1 cup water

1 cup margarine

4 tablespoons unsweetened cocoa

2 eggs

½ cup buttermilk

1 teaspoon baking soda

1 batch Easy Chocolate Frosting (see following recipe)

1. Preheat oven to 400°F. In a bowl, mix sugar, flour, and salt. Add water, margarine, and cocoa to a saucepan and bring to a boil on high heat.

2. While waiting on it to boil, add eggs, buttermilk, and baking soda to flour mixture and mix.

3. After saucepan mixture boils, pour it into bowl with remaining ingredients and mix quickly. Immediately pour it into a greased 9" x 13" pan and bake for 20 minutes or until done. Frost with Easy Chocolate Frosting and serve.

Easy Chocolate Frosting

This is the perfect frosting for Mama Randall's Chocolate Cake (see previous recipe). Both the frosting and cake are so easy to make and stir, you can do it without any electricity—no electric mixer necessary.

—Suzanne—

4 tablespoons milk

2 tablespoons margarine

2 tablespoons cocoa, unsweetened

½ box powdered sugar

Pinch of salt

Heat milk and margarine in saucepan over medium heat. Add cocoa, powdered sugar, and salt. Stir well and pour over cake.

Graham Cracker Cookie Candy

Although Mama gave me this recipe, I think it came from her friend Mrs. Sullivan. It tastes very much like candy when it is complete. Mama usually made some of these at Christmas, and I have done the same many times.

—Martha—

1 box graham crackers

3 sticks butter

1½ cups sugar

2 cups chopped nuts

1. Preheat oven to 350°F. Place crackers on greased jelly roll pan. Melt butter and sugar. Spread over crackers. Sprinkle with nuts.
2. Bake for 8–12 minutes. Watch closely because they burn easily. Immediately remove from pan and place on waxed paper or a wire rack.

Easy Crescent Chocolate Roll-Ups

Every Saturday morning in Togo, a man would ride to our house on his bike to deliver fresh Pain Chocolate (a chocolate pastry). I worked up this recipe to get the same yummy pastry taste. When Mom and Pop Pullen came to Africa, they said these chocolate pastries and the ice cream made with real cream were the best foods in Africa.

—Suzanne—

½ cup chocolate chips

1 tablespoon shortening

1 teaspoon almond extract

1 can crescent rolls

½ cup sliced almonds

Powdered sugar

1. Preheat oven to 350°F. Melt chips and shortening in microwave on high for 1–2 minutes; add almond extract and stir to combine.
2. Unroll the crescent rolls and spread with chocolate mixture. Sprinkle with almonds. Cut each in half and roll up.
3. Bake 12 minutes, remove from oven, then sprinkle with powdered sugar.

Apple Cake

When I was a cancer nurse, I once went back to visit one of my patients and gave him this cake as a gift. He was in really bad shape and had not eaten in days. His sister was there and was able to get him to start eating bites of this cake. She always said that this cake was his turning point.

—Suzanne—

2 cups sugar

1½ cups oil

2 eggs

2½ cups plain flour

2 teaspoons baking soda

1 teaspoon cloves

3 cups chopped apple

1 cup chopped pecans

1 teaspoon vanilla

1. Preheat oven to 350°F. In a medium bowl, mix sugar, oil, and eggs. Sift together flour, baking soda, and cloves, and add to first mixture. Add remaining ingredients and stir well.

2. Pour into a greased bundt pan and bake for 1 hour.

Buttermilk Pound Cake

Growing up I idolized Aunt Peg. Not only was she attractive, energetic, and an incredible homemaker, but she also led the PTA, taught aerobics, and always had time for me. At one point, she was working on starting a catering business because her cooking was always in demand. Any Aunt Peg recipe is guaranteed to be delicious!

—Suzanne—

1 cup shortening

2 cups sugar

3 cups plain flour

¼ teaspoon salt

½ teaspoon baking soda

3 eggs

1 cup buttermilk

½ teaspoon vanilla

½ teaspoon almond flavoring

1. Preheat oven to 300°F. In a medium bowl, beat together shortening and sugar until sugar is combined and mixture creamy. In a separate bowl sift together flour, salt, and baking soda 3 times. Add eggs to creamed mixture; beat to combine.
2. Alternate adding buttermilk and dry ingredients to creamed mixture. Finally, add vanilla and almond flavorings. Pour into a greased and floured bundt pan. Bake for 1½ hours. (That is not a typo—you are cooking it long and slow!)

Give thanks to the Lord, for he is good! His faithful love endures forever.

—1 CHRONICLES 16:34

Cream Cheese Blueberry Pound Cake

All the family loves it when Aunt Mary (my sister) brings goodies to all of our fam-
ily gatherings. This is the best pound cake I have ever tasted in my life. Mary has been
making it for years. I have to admit any recipe with 3 sticks of real butter and
8 ounces of cream cheese has to be good. This cake is not for dieting times but for
special occasions. She is a fantastic cook, and by the way she is very slender.
She only cooks this cake a few times each year.

—Martha—

3 sticks butter

8 ounces cream cheese

3 cups sugar

6 eggs

3 cups plain flour

1 teaspoon vanilla

1 teaspoon almond flavoring

¾ cup fresh or frozen blueberries

1. Preheat oven to 325°F. In a medium bowl, beat together butter, cream cheese, and sugar until creamy;
add eggs and mix. Stir in the flour, and add vanilla and almond.
2. Place about ½" of batter in the bottom of a greased and floured bundt pan. This will usually
prevent the blueberries from sinking to the bottom of the pan and sticking. Stir the blueberries
in the remaining batter and pour in the pan. Bake for 1 hour and 15 minutes.
(If you want it a little more done, increase baking temperature to 350°F for the last 30 minutes.)
Cake should be slightly gooey in the center. This cake freezes well.

Poppy Seed Cake

My dear friend Judy's mother, Louise Ferris, used to make this cake. She and Mr. Jimmy would drive up to the shop and bring in a warm Poppy Seed Cake for me to take home for my family. My four teenage boys would be so happy when I brought home a Miss Louise and Mr. Jimmy gift. The poppy seeds make it seem very fancy, but it is really easy to make. The cake mix in it gives you an easy shortcut to homemade goodness.

—Martha—

CAKE
1 package Duncan Hines Yellow Cake Mix

1 3-ounce box instant lemon pudding

4 tablespoons poppy seeds

1 cup water

½ cup cooking oil

4 eggs

GLAZE
⅓ cup butter, melted

1 teaspoon lemon juice

2 cups powdered sugar

1. Preheat oven to 350°F. Mix together cake mix, pudding, and poppy seeds. Add water, cooking oil, and eggs; mix well.
2. Pour into greased bundt pan. Bake 40–45 minutes. Cool for 30 minutes.
3. For the glaze, mix melted butter and lemon juice. Stir in powdered sugar until mixture is runny. Pour over cake.

Martha's Favorite Turtle Cake

Except for the Blueberry Oat Bran Muffins (see Chapter 1), I have made this cake more than any other recipe. I used to make this cake for all of the Martha Pullen sewing schools in Huntsville. I made about fifteen cakes for each school since so many people attended. If I looked in my garage, I could probably find fifteen oblong pans. I would cook each cake and freeze it right in the pan, so I had to have fifteen separate pans. I would take them to the hotel for an afternoon snack, and everyone would have a piece or two. You will love this cake, and don't tell anyone how easy it is to make. I have also purchased cans of chocolate icing to go on the top.

—Martha—

1 box German chocolate cake mix

1 14-ounce package caramel candies

¾ cup margarine

½ cup evaporated milk

12 ounces chocolate chips

1 cup pecans, chopped

Chocolate icing (optional)

1. Preheat oven to 350°F. Mix cake according to package directions. Pour half of the batter into a greased 9" x 13" pan. Bake 15 minutes. Remove from oven.
2. In a saucepan, melt caramels with margarine and milk over low heat. Pour over baked layer. Sprinkle with chocolate chips and pecans. Pour remaining half of batter over this layer and bake an additional 15–20 minutes. Frost with chocolate icing if desired.

Hot Fudge Cake

*This is one of those cakes that my mother has made often. It is so easy, and the
chocolate fudge goes well with the ice cream.*

—Suzanne—

1 cup plain flour

¾ cup sugar

2 teaspoons cocoa

2 teaspoons baking powder

½ cup milk

2 tablespoons salad oil

1 teaspoon vanilla

Nuts (optional)

1 cup brown sugar

¼ cup cocoa

1¾ cups hot water

1. Preheat oven to 350°F. Mix flour, sugar, 2 teaspoons cocoa, baking power, milk, oil, vanilla, and nuts (if using) in an 8" square baking pan.

2. In a separate bowl, mix together brown sugar, ¼ cup cocoa, and hot water. Pour hot mixture over first mixture. Bake for 45 minutes.

3. Serve hot over vanilla ice cream.

Coca-Cola Cake

This was our son Mark's favorite birthday cake when he was a child, and it still is.
It is made in a 9" x 13" pan, and we cut it right out of the pan and serve it.
It is not the fanciest cake in the world, but it is one of the best tasting.
The best way to describe it is moist and delicious.

—Martha—

CAKE		ICING
2 cups flour	½ cup buttermilk	1 stick butter
2 cups sugar	2 eggs, beaten	1 teaspoon vanilla
2 sticks butter	1 teaspoon baking soda	6 tablespoons Coca-Cola
1 cup Coca-Cola	1 teaspoon vanilla	3 tablespoons cocoa
3 tablespoons cocoa	2 cups miniature marshmallows	1 pound (one box) powdered sugar
		1 cup pecans or almonds

1. Preheat oven to 350°F.

2. For cake: In a medium bowl, combine flour and sugar, and mix well. In a saucepan, add butter, cola, and cocoa, and bring to a boil. Remove from heat and pour over flour and sugar. Add buttermilk, eggs, baking soda, and vanilla. Mix well. Then add marshmallows; stir to combine.

3. Pour into a 9" x 13" greased cake pan. Bake for 30–35 minutes. The marshmallows will rise to the top during the baking, making the cake appear a little lumpy on the top.
(Don't worry; that's the way it is supposed to look.)

4. For icing: Beat butter until light and fluffy. Add the remaining ingredients and beat well.
Pour icing over cake while it is still in the pan. Serve the cake from the pan in which it was cooked.
At our house this cake doesn't last very long.

Chocolate Pound Cake

From where we lived in Togo to Lome, where we did our grocery shopping, was a seven-hour drive. At the end of it, we would be tired and worn out, and the guest house would serve us a wonderful meal usually finished off with chocolate pound cake.

—Suzanne—

2 sticks margarine

3 cups sugar

½ cup cocoa

5 eggs

1 teaspoon vanilla

½ cup shortening

3 cups plain flour

½ teaspoon baking powder

1¼ cups milk

Preheat oven to 325°F. Combine all ingredients and mix well. Pour into a greased tube pan. Bake for 1 hour and 15 minutes.

Fabulous Microwave Fudge

I made this fudge when I got my first microwave! I was amazed that I could whip up perfect fudge every time. I will never forget that first "microwave" class I took at a local appliance store. I just could not wait to see this new marvelous appliance called a microwave oven. That night this fudge was demonstrated, and I purchased a microwave to bring home.

—Martha—

1 stick butter

1 16-ounce box powdered sugar

¼ cup milk

½ cup unsweetened cocoa powder

½ cup nuts

1 teaspoon vanilla

Microwave the butter, sugar, milk, and cocoa on high for 2 minutes. Stir well and microwave for 1 additional minute. Add the nuts and vanilla, and pour into a buttered 8" square pan.

Coconut Cake Divine

Mama always made the real thing as far as coconut cakes are concerned. Usually we had one of her spectacular four-layer cakes for Christmas. Actually my grandmother, Della Ward Campbell, whom I do not remember, always served coconut cake and little dishes of red and green Jell-O squares on Christmas day. Daddy often told the stories about their very special Christmas dessert so carefully prepared early in the 1900s. When I discovered this easy coconut cake many years ago, I could not believe how delicious it is as well as being super quick.

—Martha—

1 box Duncan Hines White Cake Mix

1 15-ounce can Coco López Cream of Coconut

1 14-ounce can sweetened condensed milk

1 16-ounce container whipped topping

1 14-ounce packet Baker's Angel Flake Coconut Sweetened
(or any sweetened, flaked coconut)

1. Prepare cake according to package directions and bake in a 13" x 9" pan. While hot, prick all over with fork. Mix cream of coconut and sweetened condensed milk.
   Pour over cake while cake is still hot. Put in refrigerator until ready to serve.

2. Before serving, spread with whipped topping and sprinkle the coconut on top. You can freeze this cake before adding the whipped topping, thaw, and top before serving. Serve cold.

Coconut Cake Divine

Dump Cake

Every autumn we take a church mission trip to the beach during a big shrimp festival. My job is usually to be the cook for the group. I always make this quick and easy dessert, and everyone raves over it. If they only knew how easy it was!

—Suzanne—

1 20-ounce can cherry pie filling

1 22-ounce can crushed pineapple

1 box yellow cake mix

1 stick butter

1. Preheat oven to 350°F. Dump cherry pie filling into a greased 9" x 13" pan.
Next add the pineapple with juice. Top that with the dry cake mix.
Chop up the butter and dot the entire top with it.
2. Bake for 45 minutes or until golden brown. Serve with whipped topping
or vanilla ice cream.

I will give thanks to the Lord because he is just;
I will sing praise to the name of the Lord Most High.

—PSALM 7:17

Penny's Pumpkin Cake

My sewing friend Penny Ackerman sent me this cake recipe. She got it from a friend in California. We love pumpkin anytime but especially during the Thanksgiving and Christmas seasons.

—Martha—

BOTTOM LAYER
1 16-ounce can pumpkin

1 12-ounce can evaporated milk

3 eggs

1½ cups sugar

1 teaspoon cinnamon

½ teaspoon pumpkin pie spice

TOP LAYER
1 box yellow cake mix

1 cup chopped pecans

2 sticks margarine

1. Preheat oven to 350°F. Mix the bottom layer ingredients well, and pour into a greased 9" x 13" pan.
2. Top with dry yellow cake mix; sprinkle pecans over top. Cut margarine into pieces and place on the very top. Bake for 45–50 minutes.

Lemon Squares

*During the citrus season in Togo, "grafted" lemons were available everywhere.
The market ladies would make a heap of five or so of these huge lemons to sell.
A heap of lemons cost around 50 cents. The season didn't last long, but at this time
we all made lots of lemon desserts and homemade lemonade.*

—Suzanne—

CRUST
1 cup butter

2⅔ cups plain flour

½ cup sugar

FILLING
4 eggs

1½ cups sugar

4 tablespoons plain flour

1 teaspoon baking powder

6 tablespoons lemon juice

Preheat oven to 350°F. Mix together crust ingredients, and press into the bottom of a 9" x 13" pan.
Bake for 15 minutes. Mix filling ingredients and pour over crust. Bake for 20 minutes.

You are good and do only good; teach me your decrees.

—PSALM 119:68

Blondies

My husband is not nearly as crazy about chocolate as I am—go figure! He loves anything vanilla. For days when you just want something different, these nutty, vanilla and brown sugar bars are a wonderful alternative to brownies.

—Suzanne—

5 tablespoons butter, softened

1 cup firmly packed brown sugar

1 teaspoon vanilla

1 egg

1 cup chopped nuts, divided

1 cup plain flour

¾ teaspoon baking powder

¼ teaspoon salt

1. Preheat oven to 350°F. In a medium bowl, beat butter and brown sugar together until sugar is combined and mixture is light and fluffy (butter should almost double in size and lighten in color).

2. Add vanilla and egg, and mix well. Mix in ¾ cup nuts.

3. In a second bowl, mix flour, baking powder, and salt. Gradually add to butter mixture.

4. Spread into a greased 8" square pan. Top with remaining nuts and bake for 30 minutes.

Twice-Baked Brownies

One of my favorite wedding presents was a set of recipe cards from my Aunt Peggy.
She was the best cook in the family. She passed away a number of years ago,
and the recipes in her handwriting have been one of my greatest treasures.
This is one of John's favorites.

—Suzanne—

FIRST LAYER
½ cup margarine (1 stick), softened

½ cup dark brown sugar

1 cup flour

SECOND LAYER
2 eggs

1 cup light brown sugar

½ cup coconut

1 cup pecans, chopped

2 tablespoons flour

1. Preheat oven to 350°F. Mix first-layer ingredients, and press into 9" square pan. Bake 20 minutes.
2. Mix second-layer ingredients, and pour over the hot first layer. Return to oven and bake an additional 15 minutes. While still hot, sprinkle with powdered sugar.

Cream Cheese Swirled Brownies

Chocolate and cream cheese together? It doesn't get any better than this!
My family loves these brownies, and they are a little bit different from the usual
brownie. Truthfully, my whole family loves brownies made any way.

—Suzanne—

CREAM CHEESE FILLING
8 ounces cream cheese, softened

¼ cup sugar

1 teaspoon cinnamon

1½ teaspoons vanilla

1 egg

BROWNIE
1 cup margarine

4 ounces unsweetened baking
chocolate

2 cups sugar

4 eggs

2 teaspoons vanilla

1½ cups plain flour

½ teaspoon salt

1 cup chopped nuts

1. Mix together all of the cream cheese filling ingredients and set aside.
2. Preheat oven to 350°F. For the brownies, in a saucepan over low heat, cook margarine and chocolate until melted. Cool.
3. In a medium bowl, beat together sugar and eggs, then add cooled chocolate mixture. Add flour, vanilla, and salt and beat for 1 minute. Fold in nuts.
4. In a greased 9" square pan, layer half of the brownie mixture, then the cream cheese filling, and top with remaining brownie mixture. Carefully swirl a spatula through the mixture to create a swirl pattern. Bake for 50–60 minutes.

Truffles

Part of the fun of Christmas is baking homemade treats for family and friends. This homemade candy recipe is perfect for filling Christmas baskets to deliver to friends and neighbors. At Christmas our whole family delivers baskets of goodies to friends and the elderly. It is amazing how many people have nothing homemade to eat at Christmas. It gives us great joy to take them our baskets made with love.

—Suzanne—

⅓ cup heavy cream

6 tablespoons butter

1 cup semisweet chocolate chips

1 cup milk chocolate chips

Cocoa powder for dusting

Chopped nuts for rolling

Extra melted chocolate for dipping

Bring cream to a simmer in a saucepan over medium heat. Cut butter into small pieces and add to cream. When melted, add both kinds of chocolate chips and stir until smooth. Remove from heat and pour into a shallow bowl. Allow to cool to room temperature. Cover and refrigerate for 2 hours. Use a melon baller to scoop.

Then I will praise God's name with singing, and I will honor Him with thanksgiving.

—PSALM 69:30

Chocolate Peanut Butter Bars

Joe loves peanut butter and thinks the perfect ending to any meal is a peanut butter cracker. I have seen him eat a delicious steak meal and later have "just a bite of peanut butter." Anytime I make him a peanut butter dessert he is a very happy camper.

—Martha—

1 cup peanut butter

6 tablespoons (¾ stick) butter, softened

1¼ cups sugar

3 eggs

1 teaspoon vanilla

1 cup flour

¼ teaspoon salt

1 11½-ounce bag milk chocolate morsels

1. Preheat oven to 350°F. Beat peanut butter and butter until smooth. Add sugar, eggs, and vanilla extract. Beat until creamy.
2. Blend in flour and salt. Stir in 1 cup milk chocolate morsels.
3. Spread into ungreased 9" x 13" baking pan. Bake for 25–30 minutes or until edges begin to brown.
4. Remove from oven and immediately sprinkle the remaining milk chocolate morsels over top. Let stand 5 minutes or until morsels become shiny and soft, then spread evenly over top.

Chess Squares

Almost every Christmas we have a get together at my sister Mary's beautiful home in Scottsboro. Our extended family always enjoys spending time together. She bakes several different kinds of goodies, and we usually play games. Family games and baked goods make for fun and tasty holiday memories.

—Martha—

CRUST
1 box yellow cake mix

1 stick butter

1 egg

FILLING
2 eggs

1 16-ounce box powdered sugar

8 ounces cream cheese

1 teaspoon vanilla

1. Preheat oven to 350°F. Mix the crust ingredients and press into a greased 9" x 13" pan. Mix the filling ingredients and pour on top of the crust.
2. Bake for 20 minutes, then turn oven down to 325°F and bake for 15 minutes.

Missionary Cookies

Missionary recipes are time-tested and simple recipes that can be easily made anywhere in the world with very few ingredients. Today, I think we have all begun to see how important it is to get back to the basics and enjoy simple things—even simple recipes! When we were missionaries in Africa, these cookies were a frequent treat for my children and their friends.

—Suzanne—

1½ cups plain flour

½ teaspoon baking powder

1 egg

½ cup margarine

½ cup sugar

¼ cup brown sugar

1 teaspoon vanilla

Preheat oven to 375°F. Mix together all ingredients. Roll out and cut into shapes. Bake 8–10 minutes.

Always be full of joy in the Lord. I say it again—rejoice!

—PHILIPPIANS 4:4

Oh Henry Chocolate Chip and Oatmeal Bars

These bars were a Togo favorite. They don't require a lot of ingredients and are wonderful to carry on trips because they don't break as easily as a cookie. When we lived in Togo, we took many, very long car trips. We laugh about driving thirty-three hours to take the girls to the mall one time. When they were little girls they had heard about malls and desperately wanted to go to one. The closest one was two countries over—literally a thirty-three-hour drive from where we lived. We drove it over several days, staying on the coast in a hotel along the way, and had a wonderful vacation visiting the mall, bowling, going out for ice cream, and enjoying the amenities of a large city. There weren't any fast-food restaurants along the way, so treats like Oh Henry bars made the drive more enjoyable.

—Suzanne—

4 cups oatmeal

1 cup margarine

1 cup sugar

½ cup brown sugar

1 cup chocolate chips, melted

½ cup peanut butter

½ cup pecans, chopped

1. Preheat oven to 350°F. Mix oatmeal, margarine, sugar, and brown sugar, and press into the bottom of a 9" x 13" greased pan to make crust. Bake crust for 12 minutes.
2. Mix together melted chocolate chips and peanut butter. Spread this mixture on hot crust. Sprinkle pecans on top. Cool and serve.

Ginger Snaps

In Togo there weren't many premade snacks, and as a result, we did a lot of baking. Ginger snaps make any time of year taste like the holidays.

—Suzanne—

⅔ cup oil

1 cup sugar

4 tablespoons molasses

1 egg

2 teaspoons baking soda

2 cups flour

1 teaspoon cinnamon

Sugar for rolling

Preheat oven to 350°F. Mix together all ingredients and roll into 1" balls.
Roll the balls in sugar and bake on a greased cookie sheet for 8–10 minutes.

For I can do everything through Christ, who gives me strength.

—PHILIPPIANS 4:13

Judy's Pecan Tassies

I think these are just the most elegant little miniature pecan pies. I love the cream cheese pastry in the little mini-muffin pans. For Christmas parties, my dear friend Judy and I made peanut blossoms and these pecan tassies. They complemented each other perfectly.

—Martha—

CRUST

3 ounces cream cheese

1 stick margarine

1 cup flour

FILLING MIX

2 medium eggs

1½ cups light brown sugar

2 tablespoons melted butter

1 teaspoon vanilla

1 cup chopped pecans

1. For crust, beat together the cream cheese and margarine until well blended. Gradually add flour at medium speed. Chill for 1 hour.

2. Form 24 balls, approximately 1" each, from chilled dough. Flour your fingers and press each ball into a miniature muffin tin, making a cup.

3. Preheat oven to 350°F. Mix together filling ingredients. Fill each cup two-thirds full. Bake for 30 minutes. Freeze after baking, if desired.

Breakfast Cookies

*This recipe was one I used when we lived in Charlotte, North Carolina.
The boys were little and sometimes balked at breakfast. (Those were the days when
we still regularly ate eggs, bacon, and sausage for breakfast.) I found this recipe
using Raisin Bran and remember the boys thinking that they were "really getting
away with something" when I let them eat cookies for breakfast.*

—Martha—

1 cup flour

¾ cup sugar

¼ teaspoon baking soda

½ cup margarine

1 egg

2 cups Raisin Bran cereal

1. Preheat oven to 350°F. Mix together flour, sugar, and baking soda. Add margarine and egg.
   Mix until all ingredients are well blended, then stir in cereal.
2. Drop by tablespoonfuls, 2" apart, on ungreased baking sheet. Bake for 13–15 minutes or
   until cookies are browned. Remove as soon as they are slightly cooled
   and place on wire rack to finish cooling.

Mother's Tea Cakes (Love in a Box Cookies)

Mama's recipe box contains a well-used recipe card written in green ink. This tattered card has the magic recipe for Nannie's sugar cookies. My grandmother, Belle Dicus, was known all over Scottsboro for her sugar cookies. When I was in college, she would bake a lot of these and carefully pack them in a box to mail to me in Tuscaloosa. Some got broken in the mail, but the crumbs were just as good as the cookies. Nannie would send these cookies fairly often since she knew we loved them so much. I now call these cookies love sent in a box.

—Martha—

1 cup sugar	2 eggs	Pinch of salt
1 cup shortening	1 teaspoon baking powder	Flour
¼ cup sweet milk (fresh, unpasteurized milk that contains live cultures)	1 teaspoon vanilla	Sugar to sprinkle on top

1. Preheat oven to 350°F. In a medium bowl, mix sugar, shortening, sweet milk, eggs, baking powder, vanilla, and salt.
2. Turn out onto a flat surface and knead as long as the dough will take flour. (This means Nannie never knew how much flour was in her cookies. She just kneaded.)
3. Roll very thin. Cut out with a round glass. Sprinkle with sugar and bake for 8–10 minutes. Be sure you don't burn them or let them get too brown. As always when making cookies, you should remove them from the pan and put onto a wire cooling rack. They get too brown and hard otherwise.

No-Bake Chocolate Oatmeal Cookies

When we lived in Togo, we all met at the pool on Friday afternoons for fun and fellowship. Rebekah was the chief cookie baker and started making these cookies in early elementary school to bring to our pool get-togethers.

—Suzanne—

2 cups sugar

1 stick margarine

½ cup milk

4 tablespoons cocoa

½ cup peanut butter

2¼ cups oatmeal

2 teaspoons vanilla

Mix sugar, margarine, and milk in saucepan over high heat. Boil for 2 minutes. Remove from heat and add remaining ingredients. Drop by spoonfuls onto wax paper and let cool.

Pumpkin Pie

The first time John was invited over for Thanksgiving, my mother asked me if she should make a pumpkin pie. We usually had chocolate and pecan pie. I told her I didn't think it was necessary. After the meal, John asked me if I wanted to go for a ride, and where did we go? Shoney's, a nearby restaurant! It wasn't Thanksgiving to him without pumpkin pie. Since then, we have never had a holiday meal without it.

—Suzanne—

¾ cup sugar

½ teaspoon salt

2 teaspoons pumpkin pie spice

2 eggs

1 15-ounce can pumpkin

1 12-ounce can evaporated milk

1 9" pie shell, unbaked

Preheat oven to 425°F. Mix together sugar, salt, pumpkin pie spice, eggs, pumpkin, and evaporated milk. Pour into pie shell. Bake for 15 minutes, then reduce oven to 350°F and bake for 45 minutes longer.

Judy's Peanut Blossoms

My dear friend Judy and I spent many days together when our children were young. We'd go to a grocery store that had chickens on sale and then run by somewhere else for their big bargains. We took our babies, Joanna and Chris, out to all the drug stores that had a $.99 photographer special. We talked on the phone about five times a day discussing recipes and dinner plans. It was glorious to have a friend like Judy as, at that time, neither of us was working outside the home. Judy's husband had just graduated from dental school, and they moved to Huntsville so he could practice dentistry with my husband, Joe. We were wives and mothers truly enjoying our babies. Judy found this recipe for peanut blossoms, and we made them over and over because everyone loved them so much.

—Martha—

1 24-ounce package chocolate kisses	½ cup brown sugar	1 teaspoon baking soda
½ cup butter	1 egg	1 teaspoon salt
½ cup peanut butter	1 teaspoon vanilla	Extra sugar for rolling cookies
½ cup sugar	1¾ cups flour	

1. Preheat oven to 375°F. Peel the chocolate kisses. In a medium bowl, beat together butter, peanut butter, sugar, and brown sugar. Add egg, vanilla, flour, baking soda, and salt. Mix well.
2. Shape into balls. Roll in sugar. Bake on an ungreased cookie sheet for 8 minutes.
3. Take out of the oven. Firmly place one kiss in the middle of each peanut blossom. Return to the oven for 2–5 minutes longer.

Togolese Coconut Cookies

In Lome, the capital of Togo, Baptists have a seminary. Some of our colleagues who taught at the seminary made these cookies for us when we had dinner with them. In Togo, fresh coconut wasn't a delicacy—it was the norm!

—Suzanne—

2 cups flour

1 teaspoon baking powder

½ teaspoon salt

1 teaspoon baking soda

1 cup firmly packed brown sugar

1 cup sugar

1 cup shortening

2 eggs

2 cups grated coconut

2 cups uncooked oatmeal

1 teaspoon vanilla

1. Preheat oven to 375°F. Sift together flour, baking powder, salt, and baking soda. Add remaining ingredients in order listed and mix well.

2. Drop onto greased baking sheet by rounded teaspoonfuls. Bake for 10–15 minutes.

Holiday Sugar Cookies

My mom makes sugar cookies for every holiday. At Christmas they have to be cut into stars and bells and carefully sprinkled with either red or green sugar. On Valentine's Day, she makes red hearts. I wanted my girls to learn how to cook early, so this was one of our first attempts. The girls were too little to comfortably reach the table from a chair, so I placed them on the table with their rolling pins and let them roll out the dough, cut it, and decorate the cookies. By the end of our first batch, the girls were covered from head to toe in flour! This is my mom's sugar cookie recipe and has always been a staple for any occasion.

—Suzanne—

3 cups flour, plain

1 teaspoon salt

½ teaspoon baking soda

1 cup butter, softened

1 cup sugar

1½ teaspoons vanilla

2 eggs

1. In one bowl, mix flour, salt, and baking soda. In another bowl, beat together butter and sugar until sugar is combined and mixture is light and fluffy (butter should almost double in size and lighten in color), then add eggs and vanilla.
2. Slowly add the flour mixture to the egg mixture. When well blended, divide into four balls and wrap tightly in wax paper. Chill overnight.
3. Preheat oven to 400°F. Take balls of dough out of refrigerator one at a time and roll out. Cut out your choice of shapes.
4. Sprinkle with sugar. Bake on ungreased cookie sheets for 8–10 minutes.

Chocolate-Topped Crispy Rice Squares

Last summer, I didn't think I could stomach one more bite of middle-school church camp food. I was the volunteer nurse for the camp, and two of my children were campers. One of the other counselors had gotten smart and brought a cooler full of fruits, vegetables, chicken salad, and so forth. On "chili dog day," she very hospitably invited me to join her for lunch in her cabin. One of the desserts in her spread was a chocolate-topped crispy rice square.

—Suzanne—

½ stick margarine

1 16-ounce bag mini marshmallows

8 cups crisp rice cereal

1 12-ounce bag chocolate chips

½ cup creamy peanut butter

1. Put margarine and marshmallows in microwave-safe bowl. Microwave on high for 2 or 3 minutes. Stir until smooth, then combine with rice cereal in a large bowl. Spread into 9" x 13" pan.
2. Melt chocolate chips in a smaller microwave-safe bowl, heating and stirring 1 minute at a time until completely melted. Stir in peanut butter, then spread on top of crisp rice mixture. Let cool for about 30 minutes before cutting.

Christine Jenkins's Cookies

Mama had this recipe carefully written out. She added the note "ships well overseas." My Uncle George served in World War II, and I think she made these cookies to send to him. Christine Finch Jenkins was my mother's half first cousin. She was a major influence in my life since I learned to sew from her and from Mama. Chris was a home economics teacher who thought everything I did in sewing was perfect. Mama was a perfectionist who taught me how to sew properly. Chris loved to make fancy food. She taught her home economics girls about beautiful things from the kitchen. I loved her so much and thank her to this day for giving me the love of sewing.

—Martha—

2 cups ground nuts

2 cups brown sugar

2 eggs

¼ teaspoon baking soda

½ teaspoon salt

1 teaspoon vanilla

3 or 4 cups flour

1. In a medium bowl, beat together ground nuts, sugar, and eggs. Add baking soda, salt, and vanilla. Work in flour until very stiff. Let stand in "icebox" 30 minutes or overnight.
2. Preheat oven to 325°F. Shape dough into 1" round balls and flatten with fork. Bake for 8–10 minutes or until brown, and remove from cookie sheet to wire cooling rack.

Mama's Icebox Peanut Cookies

I still remember these waxed paper rolls set to chill in the refrigerator. I could not wait for them to be done so Mama and I could slice and bake them.

—Martha—

¼ cup shortening

¼ cup peanut butter

2 cups dark corn syrup

1 egg

4½ cups flour, sifted

1 teaspoon cream of tartar

1 teaspoon baking soda

1 cup salted chopped peanuts (or 1 cup peanut butter)

1. Preheat oven to 400°F. In a medium bowl, beat together shortening, ¼ cup peanut butter, and dark corn syrup until creamy; beat in the egg.

2. Sift flour with the cream of tartar and baking soda. Add the chopped peanuts or peanut butter to flour mixture. Stir flour into creamed mixture. Chill slightly.

3. Place mixture on waxed paper and roll into a log. Chill in the refrigerator until firm, approximately 1 hour. Slice and bake for 10–15 minutes.

Your instructions are more valuable to me than millions in gold and silver.

—PSALM 119:72

Mama's Shortbread Cookies

Mama was a baker at heart. She loved to make cookies, especially for the holidays. She was a very careful baker, always measuring exactly. She used greater creative freedoms for seasoning casseroles and soups. These cookies are delicious and very easy to make. Be sure always to remove cookies from the baking sheet as soon as possible to cool on wire racks.

—Martha—

1 pound butter

1¼ cups light molasses

2 egg yolks

1 teaspoon vanilla

4 cups flour

1. Preheat oven to 400°F. In a medium bowl, beat together butter and molasses until creamy. Add beaten egg yolks and vanilla; mix well. Blend in flour.
2. Shape level tablespoons of dough into balls. Place on greased baking sheet, press with fork, and bake for 10 minutes. Remove as soon as possible to wire racks.

But those who obey God's word truly show how completely they love him. That is how we know we are living in him. Those who say they live in God should live their lives as Jesus did.

—1 JOHN 2:5–6

Butterscotch Cookie Cutouts

*When we lived in Togo, I did a lot of baking, especially at Christmas.
In November, we would usually get a bunch of airmail packages from
Mom Pullen loaded with all the extra goodies that we couldn't find in Togo.
John loves anything butterscotch, and so the package almost always included
the butterscotch baking morsels used in this recipe.*

—Suzanne—

1 cup butterscotch morsels

1 cup butter, softened

3 cups all-purpose flour

½ cup firmly packed brown sugar

1 egg

2 tablespoons milk

2 teaspoons vanilla

1. Melt the butterscotch morsels in a saucepan over low heat. Pour into mixing bowl and add all the remaining ingredients. Mix at low speed for 1–2 minutes. Divide dough in half, wrap each half in plastic wrap, and chill for 1 hour.

2. Preheat oven to 375°F. Roll out one ball of dough at a time on a lightly floured surface. Use cookie cutters to cut into desired shapes, and place on cookie sheet.

3. Bake for 6–8 minutes. Let cool for 1 minute, then remove from cookie sheet.

Thumbprint Cookies

The first year Joe and I were married I was asked to be the chairperson for the Ballet Garden Party sponsored by Huntsville Community Ballet. I was honored and even wore an old antebellum evening dress with a hoop skirt that I had in high school. My job was to oversee things and to make thumbprint cookies. The recipe had been in the ballet recipe file for years, and every year someone had to make them. I had never heard of thumbprint cookies much less made them, but I thought I would be up to the task. Here are the thumbprint cookies in recipe form.

—Martha—

½ cup butter

¼ cup brown sugar

1 egg plus 1 egg white

1 cup flour

¼ teaspoon salt

½ teaspoon vanilla

¾ cup finely chopped nuts

Different kinds of jelly

1. Preheat oven to 350°F. In a medium bowl, beat together butter and sugar until sugar is combined and mixture is light and fluffy (butter should almost double in size and lighten in color); add 1 egg and stir to combine.

2. In another bowl, blend together flour and salt, stir in vanilla, then add to butter-sugar-egg mixture.

3. Roll into balls (1 teaspoon per ball). Slightly beat egg white with fork. Dip balls in egg white, then roll in nuts.

4. Place about 1" apart on ungreased baking sheet; press thumb gently in center of each. Bake 10–12 minutes or until set. Cool. Fill thumbprints with jelly.

Addictive Cream Cheese Crescents

I am warning you, you won't be able to eat just one of these. John has occasionally inhaled an entire batch of these cookies. They're not too sweet, but incredibly rich. My Aunt Peg made these for my husband one Christmas and could not believe how many he ate. He absolutely fell in love with them. I have made them for him every Christmas since then. I even made them in Togo when the only cream cheese we could find came in tiny cubes that had to be painstakingly unwrapped.

—Suzanne—

8 ounces cream cheese, softened

1 cup butter, softened (2 sticks)

2 cups all-purpose flour

¼ teaspoon salt

½ cup sugar

1½ teaspoons cinnamon

¾ cup finely chopped walnuts

Powdered sugar

1. Mix together cream cheese and butter until well blended, then add flour and salt; mix to combine.
2. Divide dough into 8 equal balls, and wrap each ball in wax paper. Chill overnight.
3. Preheat oven to 350°F. Mix together sugar and cinnamon. Get one ball at a time out of the refrigerator, and roll into an 8" circle.
4. Sprinkle the circle with 1 tablespoon sugar-cinnamon mixture and 1 tablespoon chopped walnuts. Cut it into 8 pie-shaped pieces. Starting at the outside edge, roll each pie-shaped slice to the center. Repeat for remaining dough balls.
5. Place on an ungreased cookie sheet and bake for 12 minutes. While hot, dust with powdered sugar.

Holiday Cherry Cheese Bars

This recipe was one of the goodies that I baked for my open house in Mississippi. John, who was in seminary at Mid America in Memphis, was the new pastor at a small church. I thought it would be nice to invite everyone to an open house in our tiny little cottage. I cooked so many good things and got out my best tablecloth. Truly the people enjoyed it and told us over and over how much they appreciated our inviting them to our home.

—Suzanne—

CRUST
1¼ cups plain flour

½ cup packed brown sugar

½ cup margarine

1 cup walnut pieces, chopped and divided

½ cup flaked coconut

FILLING
2 8-ounce packages cream cheese

⅔ cup granulated sugar

2 eggs

2 teaspoons vanilla

1 20-ounce can cherry pie filling

1. Preheat oven to 350°F. For crust: Combine flour and brown sugar. Mix in margarine until it forms fine crumbs. Add ½ cup nuts and coconut. Mix well. Set aside ½ cup nuts-coconut mixture. Sprinkle remaining mixture into a greased 9" x 13" pan. Bake for 12 minutes.
2. For filling: While crust is cooking, beat together cream cheese, sugar, eggs, and vanilla until smooth. Pour over hot, baked crust. Return to oven and bake 15 minutes. Top with cherry pie filling. Top pie filling with ½ cup nuts-coconut mixture and ½ cup chopped nuts. Return to oven for 15 minutes longer. Refrigerate in the pan for 4 hours. Cut into bars.

So now I am giving you a new commandment: Love each other. Just as I have loved you, you should love each other.

—JOHN 13:34

Chocolate Meringue Pie

We have a tradition of allowing the birthday person to pick his or her birthday dessert. My mom always picks chocolate pie over cake. I always make this pie for Christmas and Thanksgiving as well. I knew I had received high praise indeed when Joe told me it tasted like his grandmother's pie.

—Suzanne—

1 cup sugar

2 tablespoons flour

1 tablespoon cornstarch

½ cup cocoa

1 can evaporated milk

½ cup milk

3 eggs, separated

1 teaspoon vanilla

½ stick butter

¼ teaspoon cream of tartar

6 tablespoons sugar

1 9" pie shell

1. Preheat oven to 425°F. In saucepan, whisk together sugar, flour, cornstarch, and cocoa. Gradually stir in the evaporated milk, milk, and egg yolks. When well blended, cook on medium heat until thick and bubbly, then add butter. Keep stirring constantly and cook for 2 minutes longer. Pour into prebaked pie crust.

2. In mixer, beat together egg whites and cream of tartar until peaks begin to form. Add sugar 1 tablespoon at a time and keep beating until stiff peaks form. Spread over hot filling and bake for 8 minutes.

Pecan Pie

As a preteen I didn't have a lot of money to spend on Christmas presents, but I did have time. We had a pecan tree in the yard, and my brother and I would shell pecans and package them in glass jars tied with a ribbon for presents for grandmothers and aunts. All of us loved pecan pie! I still love giving homemade food for Christmas presents. It is always appreciated.

—Suzanne—

3 eggs

2 teaspoons vanilla

½ cup sugar

¼ cup butter, melted

1 cup corn syrup

1½ cups pecans

1 9" pie shell, unbaked

Whipped cream (optional)

Preheat oven to 350°F. Beat eggs, then add remaining ingredients. Pour into pie shell and bake for 50–60 minutes. Remove from oven, cool, and garnish with whipped cream before serving if desired.

Don't just pretend to love others. Really love them. Hate what is wrong. Hold tightly to what is good. Love each other with genuine affection, and take delight in honoring each other.

—ROMANS 12:9–10

Pecan Pie

Real Chess Pie

*I may be a chocolate fiend, but John loves chess pie and vanilla desserts. I can't tell you
how glad I was to actually get his mom's chess pie recipe. Chess pie is one of those
desserts that seems decadent and difficult to make, but trust me,
it really isn't that hard. Chess pie is truly Southern!*

—Suzanne—

½ cup butter

1½ cups sugar

1 tablespoon plain cornmeal

1 teaspoon vinegar

3 eggs, beaten

5 tablespoons whole milk (skim will not do!)

1 teaspoon vanilla

9" pie shell, unbaked

1. Preheat oven to 400°F. In a medium bowl, beat margarine and sugar together until sugar is combined
   and mixture is light and fluffy (mixture should almost double in size and lighten in color).

2. In a separate bowl, mix remaining ingredients (except pie shell) well.
   Add second mixture to first mixture.

3. Pour into pie shell and bake for 10 minutes. Reduce oven temperature to 325°F and bake 25 minutes
   longer or until pie is set. To test it, insert a knife about 1" from center of pie; if it comes out clean,
   the pie is done. You can eat it slightly cooled or chilled from the refrigerator.

Martha's
Lower-Calorie Chess Pie

Joe absolutely loves this pie. In fact, he says that it is just as good as the more fattening version. To further reduce the calories, I just pull off the fluted part of the crust after the pie is baked. Joe sometimes pulls off the bottom crust, too. Of course, this "pulling" is done after the piece is served on our plates.

—Martha—

1 stick reduced-calorie margarine

1½ cups sugar substitute that pours and measures like actual sugar (I use Splenda)

1 tablespoon plain cornmeal

1 teaspoon vinegar

1 egg

4 egg whites

5 tablespoons whole milk

1 teaspoon vanilla

1 9" pie shell, unbaked

1. Preheat oven to 400°F. In a medium bowl, beat margarine and sugar substitute together until sugar is combined and mixture is light and fluffy (mixture should almost double in size and lighten in color).
2. In a separate bowl, mix remaining ingredients well. Add second mixture to first mixture.
3. Pour into pie shell. Bake for 10 minutes. Reduce temperature to 325°F and bake for 25 minutes longer or until set. To test, insert knife about 1" from center; pie is finished if knife comes out clean.

Always be humble and gentle. Be patient with each other, making allowance for each other's faults because of your love.

—EPHESIANS 4:2

Chocolate Chip Pie

I have probably made several hundred of these pies in my life. It is a quick, easy, and delicious dessert! When I don't have any chocolate chips on hand, I sometimes chop up a chocolate bar instead. My daughter Rebekah loves to make this dessert. If we need to bring dessert to any gathering, she begs to be allowed to make this treat. It is requested at all of our family Thanksgiving and Christmas meals to go on the dessert buffet!

—Suzanne—

2 eggs

½ cup sugar

½ cup brown sugar

¾ cup butter, softened

½ cup flour

2 teaspoons vanilla

1 cup semisweet chocolate chips

1 cup chopped pecans

1 9" pie shell, unbaked

1. Preheat oven to 325°F. Beat together eggs, sugars, butter, flour, and vanilla until frothy. Stir in nuts and chocolate chips.

2. Pour into pie crust and bake for 50 minutes or until knife inserted halfway to center comes out clean. Serve with a scoop of vanilla ice cream.

Quick and Easy Fruit Cobbler

One of the benefits of being a rural pastor's wife in Hernando, Mississippi, was that everyone shared their garden with you. One of our parishioners had blueberry bushes and would invite us to come pick some fairly often. They were wonderful for making jelly and for this fruit cobbler!

—Suzanne—

1 cup self-rising flour

1 cup sugar

1 cup milk

1 stick margarine, softened

2 cups chopped fruit or 1 20-ounce can pie filling

Preheat oven to 350°F. Mix together all ingredients except fruit. Pour into greased 8" x 8" pan. Top with fruit or pie filling. Do not stir! Bake for 45 minutes.

You were cleansed from your sins when you obeyed the truth, so now you must show sincere love to each other as brothers and sisters. Love each other deeply with all your heart.

—1 PETER 1:22

Thelma's Chocolate Pecan Pie

Thelma was one of my grandmother's friends. She always made this incredible chocolate pecan pie for various gatherings. We all thought it had to be a very complicated recipe until she shared just how easy it is.

—Suzanne—

¼ cup butter

1 5-ounce can evaporated milk

1½ cups sugar

3 tablespoons cocoa

2 eggs, beaten

1 teaspoon vanilla

½ cup chopped pecans

1 9″ pie shell, unbaked

Preheat oven to 300°F. Melt butter; pour into medium bowl. Add milk, sugar, and cocoa; stir to combine. Add eggs, vanilla, and pecans; stir to combine. Pour into pie shell. Bake for 40 minutes.

Your eternal word, O Lord, stands firm in heaven. Your faithfulness extends to every generation, as enduring as the earth you created.

—PSALM 119:89–90

Aunt Peg's Coconut Pie

Anything Aunt Peg cooked was delicious. Her pies were no exception! When we stayed at her house, her daughters graciously gave up their bedrooms for us. One night we had been playing with the toys in the girls' room and had inadvertently set a child's alarm clock. My parents were sleeping in that room when at 2:00 A.M. Big Bird began shouting, "It's time to get up! Wash your face and brush your teeth!" It was very loud and wouldn't stop. We had to dump out the entire toy box before we found it and could all go back to sleep. Having relatives come stay with you may be inconvenient, but it can also make for great family memories.

—Suzanne—

PIE FILLING
2 pie crusts

1½ cups sugar

4 tablespoons cornstarch

3 cups milk

4 egg yolks

1 cup coconut

1 teaspoon vanilla

2 tablespoons butter

MERINGUE
4 egg whites

¼ teaspoon cream of tartar

6 tablespoons sugar

1. Preheat oven to 425°F. Bake pie crusts for 8 minutes.
2. In heavy pan, whisk together sugar and cornstarch. Gradually whisk in milk and egg yolks, and cook on low heat, stirring constantly. Leave on low heat until mixture starts to boil. This takes time but the filling will boil. When mixture starts to boil add coconut, vanilla, and butter, and whisk for 2 minutes longer. Remove from heat and pour into pie crusts. Keep oven at 425°F.
3. Meringue: Beat egg whites and cream of tartar at high speed until soft peaks form. Add sugar while beating until stiff peaks form. Put meringue on hot pies and bake for 10 minutes or until lightly browned.

Vinegar Pie

As a young pastor's wife cooking on a budget, I often turned to this recipe as one of my potluck staples. Don't let the name discourage you from trying it. This really is a tart, delicious pie. You have to know you are reading a Southern cookbook when you see a recipe for something called Vinegar Pie! Enjoy!

—Suzanne—

4 eggs

1½ cups sugar

¼ cup butter, melted

1½ tablespoons cider or white vinegar

1 teaspoon vanilla extract

1 9" pie shell, unbaked

Preheat oven to 350°F. Mix eggs, sugar, butter, vinegar, and vanilla, and pour into pie shell. Bake for 45–55 minutes or until set in center.

Egg Custard Pie

When my grandfather was elderly and had a difficult time eating, my mother made one of these pies almost every day for him. This cool, creamy dessert is the ultimate comfort food, and the eggs and milk provided much-needed nourishment for my grandfather.

—Martha—

3 eggs

1 cup sugar

3 tablespoons flour

2 tablespoons butter

1 tablespoon vanilla

1 12-ounce can evaporated milk

Nutmeg

Preheat oven to 350°F. Blend all ingredients well, except nutmeg, and pour into a buttered and floured 9" pie pan. Sprinkle with nutmeg and bake for 30–35 minutes. Chill before serving.

Martha's All-Time Favorite Apple Pie

This apple, cream cheese, and caramel candy pie is my favorite pie in the world. I have to admit I have changed the recipe from the original version that I found many years ago. This is my version, and I hope you enjoy it.

—Martha—

CARAMEL TOPPING	PASTRY	APPLE PIE FILLING	CREAM CHEESE TOPPING
28 light-colored candy caramels	3 cups sifted flour	6 cups peeled, sliced apples (about 6 apples)	8 ounces cream cheese
½ cup evaporated milk	¼ cup sugar	1 cup sugar	1 egg
	1½ teaspoons salt	½ cup flour	⅓ cup sugar
	½ cup butter	2 teaspoons grated lemon rind	
	¼ cup cooking oil	3 tablespoons lemon juice	
	1 egg		
	¼ cup cold water		

1. **For Caramel Topping:** Melt caramels and evaporated milk in a double boiler or in the microwave, stirring often. Keep warm.

2. **For Pastry:** Mix flour, sugar, and salt in a bowl. Cut in butter until particles are fine. In a separate bowl, blend oil, egg, and cold water until smooth. Add wet mixture to dry ingredients. Stir until the mixture holds together. Roll out to about 18" x 12" and place on cookie sheet. Push up on the sides to form a rim around the pastry.

3. **For Filling:** In a medium bowl, combine apples, sugar, flour, lemon rind, and lemon juice, tossing to coat the apples. Spread apples out over the pastry in the cookie sheet.

4. **For Topping:** Preheat oven to 375°F. Beat together cream cheese, egg, and sugar until smooth. Alternate drizzling the cream cheese topping with the warm caramel topping in about 2" strips. I like to drizzle at an angle rather than straight across the pie. If you like, sprinkle with pecans before baking. Bake for 30–35 minutes until lightly browned. This pie is fabulous hot or cold.

Brown Bag Apple Pie

I always enjoyed this pie when I was growing up as a pastor's daughter in Guatemala, where we were missionaries, and then in Georgia. My mother was a very creative cook. It never ceased to amaze me that something so tasty could come out of a paper sack! If you have a hard time with the edges of your crust burning, this is the recipe to try. The bag keeps it from getting overdone.

—Suzanne—

4 cups peeled and pared tart apples

½ cup sugar

2 tablespoons flour

2 teaspoons cinnamon

1 9" pie shell, unbaked

TOPPING

¾ stick margarine

½ cup plain flour

½ cup sugar

1. Preheat oven to 425°F. Mix apples, ½ cup sugar, 2 tablespoons flour, and cinnamon, and pour into pie shell.
2. Mix together topping ingredients until crumbly; sprinkle on top of pie. Place whole pie into a paper bag and staple shut. Cook for 30 minutes, then reduce temperature to 375°F and bake for 35 minutes.

Lemonade Pie

I often make this quick and easy dessert at Christmas or Thanksgiving. It is so easy to make ahead of time and tastes like you spent hours working on it. My daughter, Joanna, often makes this ice cream/lemonade pie when she has people over to their lake place in the summer. I always made it at Christmas just in case someone did not want all of the rich desserts that were on the desert buffet. To be truthful, my family prefers the more traditional desserts during Christmas and Thanksgiving meals. I have to remember that I am the "ice cream girl," and I always like anything resembling good ice cream.

—Martha—

1 6-ounce can frozen lemonade (or limeade)

½ gallon vanilla ice cream

2 8" graham cracker crusts

Sliced almonds (optional)

Whipped cream (optional)

Soften lemonade and ice cream. (I put the ice cream into a blender to soften it.) Beat together until creamy. Pour into graham cracker crusts and freeze until serving time. Sprinkle the top with sliced almonds and a dollop of whipped cream if you like. I always put the plastic lids from the graham cracker crusts on top of the pies and seal the little foil pie dish around this plastic top. This keeps it from getting freezer burn if you are going to leave it in the freezer for several days.

Finally, all of you should be of one mind. Sympathize with each other. Love each other as brothers and sisters. Be tenderhearted, and keep a humble attitude.

—1 PETER 3:8

Lemon Chess Pie

As Southerners, we really like chess pie. Some of you might never have heard of this very rich, very delicious pie. When the School of Art Fashion students come to our house for the barbecue, we have many varieties of homemade pies from Gibson's, a wonderful restaurant in Huntsville, and a chess pie is usually one of them. Mama always made egg custard pies and chess pies for my daddy and my granddaddy since they were their favorites. After reading a few of these family recipes, you probably don't wonder why I am a little fluffy around the middle.

—Martha—

4 eggs

2 cups sugar

½ cup milk

6 tablespoons butter, melted

1 tablespoon plain flour

1 tablespoon corn meal

Juice and rind of 2 lemons

2 9" pie shells, unbaked

1. Preheat oven to 350°F. Beat eggs well; add sugar, milk, and melted butter.

2. Add flour, corn meal, and lemon juice and rind. Pour into pie shell.

3. Bake for 1 hour or until done. You'll know it's done when the top is brown.

Easy Cherry Cheese Pie

My senior year in high school, I was asked to do a teaching project. I don't remember what my project was, but a male friend did a baking demonstration and made cheesecake. I still remember how incredibly complicated it all was. This recipe gives you the taste of a complicated cheesecake with a fraction of the work!

—Suzanne—

8 ounces cream cheese, softened

1 14-ounce can condensed milk

½ cup lemon juice

1 teaspoon vanilla extract

1 9" graham cracker crust

1 20-ounce can cherry pie filling

1. Beat cream cheese until fluffy. Gradually beat in condensed milk, lemon juice, and vanilla.
2. Pour into pie crust and chill for 3 hours. Just before serving, top with cherry pie filling.

You will show me the way of life, granting me the joy of your presence and the pleasures of living with you forever.

—PSALM 16:11

Pumpkin Layer Cheesecake

*If you want a different take on pumpkin pie for the holidays,
this cheesecake is worth the effort. It combines two of the best holiday
tastes—cheesecake and pumpkin—into one elegant dessert.*

—Suzanne—

2 8-ounce packages cream cheese, softened

2 eggs

½ cup sugar

½ teaspoon vanilla

½ cup canned pumpkin

1 teaspoon pumpkin pie spice

1 9" graham cracker crust

1. Preheat oven to 350°F. Beat cream cheese, eggs, sugar, and vanilla until fluffy.
2. In another bowl, mix pumpkin and spices with 1 cup of the batter. Pour remaining plain batter into crust. Top with pumpkin mixture. Bake for 35–40 minutes. Chill overnight.

Aunt Scottie's Trifle

*One of our furlough highlights was to visit John's Aunt Scottie in Asheville.
We would spend the day in the mountains hiking and swimming and come home to a
delicious meal she would prepare at night. Trifle was always her signature dessert, and
once she shared her secret as to how easy it is to make, we've had it for
many of our summer celebrations.*

—Suzanne—

1 store-bought angel food cake

1 7-ounce box vanilla pudding, prepared according to directions

16 ounces strawberries, sliced

4 ounces blueberries

2 or 3 bananas, sliced

5 or 6 kiwi fruit, peeled and sliced

2 16-ounce containers whipped topping

Tear cake into small pieces. In bottom of trifle dish, place layer of cake pieces. Layer some of the
pudding, the fruit, and then the whipped topping; repeat three times. Garnish with strawberries.
I always line up the strawberries and kiwi along the outside edge of the trifle to make it look pretty.
You can lighten it up with light pudding and whipped topping.

Honor and majesty surround him; strength and joy fill his dwelling.

—1 CHRONICLES 16:27

Baked Banana Pudding with Meringue

Baked Banana Pudding with Meringue

Growing up, this was one of my favorite desserts. It takes a little time and effort, but it is night and day different from packaged pudding mixes. For a special Sunday meal, it is well worth it! My brother-in-law, Ron, says this homemade banana pudding is one of the most Southern of all dishes. His mother always made homemade banana pudding for her children for special occasions.

—Suzanne—

4 tablespoons plain flour

2 cups plus 6 tablespoons sugar

3½ cups milk

3 eggs, separated

Dash salt

1 teaspoon vanilla

¼ teaspoon cream of tartar

1 box vanilla wafers

6 bananas

1. In a heavy saucepan, whisk together flour and 2 cups sugar. Pour in milk, egg yolks, and dash salt. Whisk together and cook on medium heat until thick and bubbly. Add vanilla. Let sit and cool.

2. Beat egg whites and cream of tartar until peaks begin to form. Gradually add 6 tablespoons of sugar and keep beating until firm peaks form.

3. Preheat oven to 400°F.

4. Place a layer of vanilla wafers in an oven-safe casserole dish. Put them all the way up the sides of the dish. Slice up bananas and add them as the next layer. Next, pour the cooled custard. Finally, spoon the meringue on top. Bake for 10 minutes or until browned. Serve warm or cool.

NEW YEAR'S FEAST

—Suzanne—

So if we have enough food and clothing, let us be content.

—1 TIMOTHY 6:8

It was New Year's Eve, and my house help was leaving for the day. "You know that you will have a lot of visitors tomorrow, don't you?" she called out as she changed from her work clothes into street clothes. I was clueless. I asked her to explain what she meant, and she told me that the New Year's tradition was that everyone ate at all their friends' homes on New Year's Day. She went on to explain that we now had lots of friends and acquaintances and that they would come by early so I should be prepared with food and gifts.

I had a momentary panic. Where would I get enough food? Then I got to work. The first thing I had to do was to run to the market. Unfortunately, it was late in the day so there wasn't any meat for sale, but I was able to get lots of rice, noodles, and peanut butter. I imagine that sounds like a bizarre combination to you. In the United States, we don't cook much rice and peanut butter together, but you would be surprised at how tasty peanut sauce is over rice. Then I went by the ice cream store and bought 200 popsicles for the children who would

be coming by our house to wish us a happy New Year. When I got home, I began defrosting all the meat in the freezer. I got up early the next morning and made 2 gallons of sauce and a huge amount of rice and noodles. I felt like I was prepared.

Before 7 A.M., people began to arrive. The first arrivals ate quickly and left, but word soon spread that we were participating in the neighborhood feast ritual. We set up a TV with the "Jesus" film playing so people could watch, and we gave out Gospel tracts as gifts for our visitors. I kept frantically washing bowls, cooking food and serving visitors all morning long while John talked to all our guests. Children rang the bell by the gate and brought us elaborately colored New Year's cards they had made, and we gave them popsicles in return. It was a wonderful day of getting to know our neighbors better and being able to share the Gospel with some people who had previously been closed. At the end of the day, we counted up and realized that we had fed about 200 adults and 175 kids.

The next year we were better prepared. Word was passed to us through the grapevine that people didn't want Togolese food at our house. They wanted American food. So that year I made several hundred egg-salad sandwiches. They were a big hit. I changed the recipe a bit and added Dijon mustard, hot pepper, and onions to make it more palatable to people who like food spicy. My girls were big enough that year to go on the rounds of eating at their friends' houses along with the other missionary kids. We had to laugh at one gluttonous child who collapsed on the floor saying, "I ate duck, goat, sheep, cow, and chicken. I ate spaghetti, rice, couscous, fou fou (pounded yams), millet (a grain that is ground and cooked as a porridge), and pate (another porridge eaten with spicy sauce). I think I'm going to die!" His tummy ache proved to be nonfatal, and he did recover well after a long nap.

One of our last visitors that year was an older woman. I asked her to tell me more about this New Year's tradition. Why this frenzy of eating and drinking from house to house? She became very serious for a minute in the midst of the hilarity of the day and said, "Because we had enough food this year, and we did not die." Under all the frenzy was a sense of gratitude for something as basic as food and life.

Tell Your Story

1. Make a list of at least ten things you are thankful for right now. Then write about how that list might have been different twenty years ago. _____

_____

_____

_____

2. How have you celebrated or not celebrated New Year's Eve through the years? _____

_____

_____

_____

THE POTPOURRI SNACK

—Suzanne—

Finally, all of you should be of one mind. Sympathize with each other. Love each other as brothers and sisters. Be tenderhearted, and keep a humble attitude.

—1 PETER 3:8

In December 1991, I was a young preacher's wife living in Hernando, Mississippi. I had tried leading a daytime women's Bible study, but that flopped. Most of the women in the church worked outside the home during the day and were unable to attend. I sang in the choir, but I certainly wasn't a soloist. I didn't play an instrument. I felt like I was helping here and there, but I was struggling to find my niche. My seminary pastor's wife class had taught me that a pastor's wife should always host a Christmas open house, so I decided that was what I would do. Never mind the fact that we lived in a tiny "dollhouse" or that no one in Hernando hosted open house parties. The book said I should, and so I would.

I set about collecting all kinds of holiday recipes, including the Holiday Cherry Cheese Bars in this chapter. I cleaned the house within an inch of its life and baked up a storm. When the evening arrived I was nervous and afraid that no one would come, but the church members came by droves. Many brought us homemade Christmas ornaments as gifts, and I still hang them on the tree every year. To make sure everything smelled good, I set out a bowl of cinnamon potpourri in the middle of the table. Everyone ate their fill and seemed to have a good time visiting.

As I was telling my guests goodnight, precious ninety-five-year-old Meemaw Kelly stopped to tell me how much she had enjoyed everything. "The snacks were delicious, except for that bowl in the middle. It tasted a little like sawdust." The bowl in the middle was my potpourri! The end result of that party was much closer fellowship and the beginning of a relationship with Meemaw Kelly. She took me under her wing and shared strawberry plants, gardening knowledge, recipes, and a lot of love with this city girl. Her friendship and words of wisdom helped me adjust to my new role in a rural setting.

Tell Your Story

1. Can you remember a time when you had to cook something for work or for your child's school? Did anything funny or memorable happen? If not, just write down what you fixed and carried.

_____

_____

_____

_____

_____

_____

_____

_____

_____

_____

_____

2. What is the funniest thing that you have ever seen happen at a potluck?

_____

_____

_____

_____

_____

_____

_____

_____

_____

_____

_____

APPENDIX A

"Tell Your Own Story" Memory Pages

As we've discussed throughout the book, food plays such an important role in our memories of family picnics, baby showers, holidays, and just about anything else you can think of! And hopefully the recipes, prompts, and memories that we've shared with you throughout the book have you thinking about your own family recipes and the memories that go along with them!

In this section, it's time for you to take the memories that the writing prompts throughout the book have reignited and start to compile a list of the recipes that go along with them. For example, maybe every time you take a bite of the mac and cheese that you made with your grandmother's recipe you remember the first time you made and served it in your own home. Or maybe you remember eating that amazing chocolate cake that your mama is famous for every time you went over to her house to celebrate a holiday or special occasion. In the pages that follow, write down these memories and the recipes that go along with them. Don't worry if it isn't neat and organized. Preserving these memories and recipes is important, and here you're taking the first step toward guaranteeing that your children, grandchildren, and future generations will be able to hold onto the recipes and family history that mean so much to you. So grab your pen and get started!

Thank you for making me so wonderfully complex!
Your workmanship is marvelous—how well I know it.

—PSALM 139:14

_____
_____
_____
_____
_____
_____
_____
_____
_____
_____

Remember the things I have done in the past. For I alone am God!
I am God, and there is none like me.

—ISAIAH 46:9

_____
_____
_____
_____
_____
_____
_____
_____
_____
_____

Your unfailing love is better than life itself; how I praise you!

—PSALM 63:3

_____
_____
_____
_____
_____
_____
_____
_____
_____
_____
_____
_____

Christ is the same yesterday, today, and forever.

—HEBREWS 13:8

_____
_____
_____
_____
_____
_____
_____
_____
_____
_____
_____
_____
_____

And now, dear brothers and sisters, one final thing. Fix your thoughts on what is true, and honorable, and right, and pure, and lovely, and admirable. Think about things that are excellent and worthy of praise.

—PHILIPPIANS 4:8

APPENDIX B
Measurement Conversion Chart

VOLUME CONVERSIONS

U.S. Volume Measure	Metric Equivalent
⅛ teaspoon	0.5 milliliters
¼ teaspoon	1 milliliters
½ teaspoon	2 milliliters
1 teaspoon	5 milliliters
½ tablespoon	7 milliliters
1 tablespoon (3 teaspoons)	15 milliliters
2 tablespoons (1 fluid ounce)	30 milliliters
¼ cup (4 tablespoons)	60 milliliters
⅓ cup	90 milliliters
½ cup (4 fluid ounces)	125 milliliters
⅔ cup	160 milliliters
¾ cup (6 fluid ounces)	180 milliliters
1 cup (16 tablespoons)	250 milliliters
1 pint (2 cups)	500 milliliters
1 quart (4 cups)	1 liter (about)

WEIGHT CONVERSIONS

U.S. Weight Measure	Metric Equivalent
½ ounce	15 grams
1 ounce	30 grams
2 ounces	60 grams
3 ounces	85 grams
¼ pound (4 ounces)	115 grams
½ pound (8 ounces)	225 grams
¾ pound (12 ounces)	340 grams
1 pound (16 ounces)	454 grams

OVEN TEMPERATURE CONVERSIONS

Degrees Fahrenheit	Degrees Celsius
200 degrees F	95 degrees C
250 degrees F	120 degrees C
275 degrees F	135 degrees C
300 degrees F	150 degrees C
325 degrees F	160 degrees C
350 degrees F	180 degrees C
375 degrees F	190 degrees C
400 degrees F	205 degrees C
425 degrees F	220 degrees C
450 degrees F	230 degrees C

BAKING PAN SIZES

American	Metric
8 x 1½ inch round baking pan	20 x 4 cm cake tin
9 x 1½ inch round baking pan	23 x 3.5 cm cake tin
11 x 7 x 1½ inch baking pan	28 x 18 x 4 cm baking tin
13 x 9 x 2 inch baking pan	30 x 20 x 5 cm baking tin
2 quart rectangular baking dish	30 x 20 x 3 cm baking tin
15 x 10 x 2 inch baking pan	30 x 25 x 2 cm baking tin (Swiss roll tin)
9 inch pie plate	22 x 4 or 23 x 4 cm pie plate
7 or 8 inch springform pan	18 or 20 cm springform or loose bottom cake tin
9 x 5 x 3 inch loaf pan	23 x 13 x 7 cm or 2 lb narrow loaf or pate tin
1½ quart casserole	1.5 liter casserole
2 quart casserole	2 liter casserole

ABOUT THE AUTHORS

MARTHA CAMPBELL PULLEN started her sewing business in a tiny shop in Huntsville, Alabama, and now, more than thirty years later, she conducts full-scale Martha Pullen sewing schools in Australia, England, Sweden, Canada, and New Zealand, as well as forty-six states. Martha is the founder of *Sew Beautiful* magazine and has authored over fifty-five books in the sewing arena. Martha also earned a PhD in educational administration and management and was inducted into the American Sewing Guild Hall of Fame and named a national Daughter of Distinction of the Daughters of the American Revolution. She's also been named Huntsville/Madison County Chamber of Commerce Executive of the Year, the second woman in the history of the organization to receive this award. Wife of Joe Ross Pullen, DMD, mother of five, and grandmother to eighteen, Martha is an active member of her church, Whitesburg Baptist, and has volunteered with the Southern Baptist International Mission Board in Africa, Jamaica, and Brazil. A devoted Christian, Martha gives the credit for her sewing business and all of her other blessings to God. Martha lives in Huntsville, Alabama. Check her out at *www.marthapullen.com*.

SUZANNE CROCKER received a nursing degree from Samford University and achieved her childhood dream to be a nurse missionary in Africa when she married John Crocker and they served in Togo and Benin for ten years with the International Mission Board of the Southern Baptist Church. Suzanne is currently finishing her degree as a nurse practitioner, but she loves speaking to Christian women's groups. Suzanne has always loved to cook and still cooks a meal every day for her family. Suzanne lives with her husband and four children in Huntsville, Alabama.

SOFTWARE LICENSE AGREEMENT